WE HAVE A POPE!
BENEDICT XVI

Matthew E. Bunson, D.Min.

WE HAVE A POPE!
BENEDICT XVI

Matthew E. Bunson, D.Min.

Our Sunday Visitor Publishing Division
Our Sunday Visitor, Inc.
Huntington, Indiana 46750

The Scripture citations contained in this work are taken from the *Catholic Edition of the Revised Standard Version of the Bible* (RSV), copyright © 1965 and 1966 by the Division of Christian Education of the National Council of the Churches of Christ in the United States of America. Used by permission. All rights reserved.

Every reasonable effort has been made to determine copyright holders of excerpted materials and to secure permissions as needed. If any copyrighted materials have been inadvertently used in this work without proper credit being given in one form or another, please notify Our Sunday Visitor in writing so that future printings of this work may be corrected accordingly.

Copyright © 2005 by Our Sunday Visitor Publishing Division,
Our Sunday Visitor, Inc. Published 2005
10 09 08 07 06 05   1 2 3 4 5 6 7 8 9

All rights reserved. With the exception of short excerpts for critical reviews, no part of this work may be reproduced or transmitted in any form or by any means whatsoever without permission in writing from the publisher. Write:

Our Sunday Visitor Publishing Division
Our Sunday Visitor, Inc.
200 Noll Plaza
Huntington, IN 46750

ISBN: 1-59276-180-1 (Inventory No. T231)
LCCN: 2005926840

Cover design by Rebecca J. Heaston
Cover photo by Kai Pfaffenbach, courtesy of Reuters/Corbis
Interior design by Sherri L. Hoffman

PRINTED IN THE UNITED STATES OF AMERICA

POPE BENEDICT XVI

Pope Benedict XVI

Born Joseph Ratzinger
April 16, 1927
Marktl am Inn, Germany

Ordained Priest
June 29, 1951

Ordained Archbishop of Munich-Freising
May 28, 1977

Created Cardinal
June 27, 1977

Elected Pope
April 19, 2005

Prayer for Pope Benedict XVI

————✠————

*Lord Jesus Christ, you have chosen your servant
Pope Benedict XVI to lead your Church. By your Holy Spirit
now confirm him, we pray, in faith, hope, and love. Grant him
grace to work in the vineyard of the Lord with wisdom and
courage. Pour out your Spirit upon all your people as we join
him in seeking the will of God the Father. Amen.*

CONTENTS

FOREWORD

✠

In Appreciation of Our New Pope

With four quick votes in less than 24 hours, 115 Cardinals confounded weeks of debate and speculation, moving with remarkable speed to select the 265th Pope of the Catholic Church.

Perhaps the most quoted line in speculative analyses preceding the conclave was the Roman saying, "He who goes into the conclave a Pope, comes out a Cardinal." As I wrote during that historic week in Rome, however, this saying is true, except when it isn't. Indeed, the man who went into the conclave Pope, came out Pope: Cardinal Joseph Ratzinger, dean of the College of Cardinals, Prefect for the Congregation of the Faith, and perhaps Pope John Paul II's closest collaborator in all matters theological, doctrinal and disciplinary, is now Pope Benedict XVI.

For many churchmen, journalists and authors, there is a feeling that Pope Benedict is a known quantity, the opposite of the feeling when Pope John Paul II was elected. As Cardinal Ratzinger, he was a man that many of us have known in one capacity or another. He has been a major figure in the Church for nearly 25 years. We have seen him, written about him, read his writings, debated his decisions, perhaps even encountered him during his solitary daily commute from his apartment near the Vatican across St. Peter's Square to the Holy Office.

Certainly, he will be a sign of continuity simply because he is Pope and because he shared in many ways John Paul II's vision of the Church.

Despite the exaggerated desires of some, the papal job description does not include being a revolutionary. The mission of the office is to

11

preserve and teach, not speculate and overturn. The political language of "conservative" and "progressive," "right wing" and "left wing," misses the fact that the papacy is first and foremost about continuity. If one wants to appreciate the reign of Paul VI, look to John XXIII. If one wants to appreciate the reign of John Paul II, look to Paul VI and John Paul I. So it will be, at least in part, with this papacy.

Yet there is a great temptation to see Pope Benedict as the accumulation of news events and controversies about the pontificate of Pope John Paul II. I think that it would be unfair to adopt without challenge the media's stereotypes regarding our new Pope. In truth, even as head of the doctrinal congregation, he was known for his courtesy as well as for his monumental intellectual abilities. U.S. Cardinal Theodore McCarrick described him as both "a genius" and "a very spiritual man." Despite the near hysterical comments by a few of his critics, he has not been a grand inquisitor. Instead, he has treated theologians fairly and with consideration even while being calmly insistent that they remain faithful to divine revelation and the core teachings of the faith.

In his first days as Pope, I think we are seeing some of these same traits. He has reached out to other Christians and to non-Christians. He has been strikingly humble in his public speeches, invoking often the memory of his "revered predecessor," and making it clear that his agenda will be in large part a pursuit of the priorities established by John Paul.

Yet he has also used each public encounter as an opportunity to supply moving spiritual reflections and to teach a little about the faith as well. While it was widely noted that he met with the world's news media on April 23 in the Paul VI Hall at the Vatican, for example, only a few participants appreciated the fact that he began his encounter with the world media with the Sign of the Cross and ended it with a recitation of the Our Father. In the homily at his Mass of Installation the next day, he did an extensive catechesis on the scriptural foundations of the papacy rather than outlining his new agenda.

This is Pope as teacher, even Pope as catechist, and if he may not have as public a papacy as his predecessor, he will be no less focused on the responsibility of his office to communicate the essence of the faith to all who will listen.

This is also a man who, as a Western European, has seen the rise and fall of two great "isms" — fascism and communism — and now sees the West apparently succumbing to materialistic consumerism and to what he calls the "dictatorship of relativism," that is, the lonely subjectivity of the individual who must make his way through the world without moral truth or divine hope.

It is a geographical irony that in Pope John Paul II we had the "Apostle from the East," a son of Poland and one who survived the Nazi terror and helped to overthrow the Communist dictatorship that followed. Now, from neighboring Germany, the source of Nazism and a country divided by Communism for 50 years, comes the "Apostle from the West," Pope Benedict, to face an even more tenacious foe. He has thought a great deal about the predicament of modern human beings, and he firmly believes that only the Church offers a true alternative to the moral stagnation that seems to characterize modern consumer societies.

For all of these reasons, the selection of the name Benedict is significant.

First, he has signalled that he will be his own man, not just a caretaker, although he clearly sees himself as a direct descendant of the mission and vision of John Paul.

Second, his personal devotion to St. Benedict, the founder of Western monasticism and a great saint of both prayer and spiritual discipline, reflects his own spiritual priorities.

Finally, the Pope most certainly appreciates the fact that Benedict is the co-patron of Europe. The monastic world he founded in time became the guardian of all the best of Western culture, preserving it for centuries, as well as giving the Church some of its greatest leaders, including St. Gregory the Great.

In choosing a western European with such a devotion, the conclave fathers were affirming that the Church's struggle for the soul of the West — for Europe and for America — is not lost. Yes, the Third World is critical for the Church. The internationalization of the Church Universal will continue. But if Christianity is to obey its evangelical mandate, then it must not throw in the towel on those societies where consumerism and moral relativism are most dominant, or the future will be lost as Asian, Latin American, and African societies grow in wealth and opportunity.

What will Pope Benedict mean for Catholic Americans? First, as our new Pope, he certainly deserves our obedience as well as our affection. The cult of celebrity that surrounds modern Popes can obscure the fact that he is the leader of the Church, and not just a benevolent, grandfatherly figure.

Because he is from one of the richest and most developed nations in the world, one in which the Church has struggled to maintain its presence in society, he will no doubt appreciate the relative vitality of America's Catholics even as he understands the challenges posed to their faith. He also appreciates the religious freedoms of this country, and the religious diversity that has developed.

I think that those who are frustrated by a certain blurring of our Catholic identity, particularly younger Catholics, are likely to find in Pope Benedict — as they did in John Paul II — a leader who will encourage a rediscovery of Catholicism's intellectual and spiritual roots. He wants Catholics to know who they are and what their mission is.

Above all else, Pope Benedict exudes confidence in the revelation of Jesus Christ and the indispensable role of the Church in spreading the good news of the Gospel. He appreciates with depth and passion the mercy of God and, in the words of his final homily as a Cardinal, the "friendship of Jesus."

Pope Benedict may be the last Pope to have played an important role in the Second Vatican Council, for he is one of the few surviving theologians who helped to shape that council 40 years ago, and he has stressed his desire to continue the work of its implementation.

Yet he is also the first Pope elected in the third millennium, and he will be speaking to 21st century men and women facing the challenges of today. He will bring to the task of leading the Catholic Church the insights of more than 50 years of theological reflection. He also becomes Pope after having served 25 years in the Vatican Curia. He knows the leaders of the Church around the world, and he knows the problems they face.

Pope Benedict's learning curve will be short, and his impact is likely to be profound and perhaps surprising. We pray that Catholics everywhere embrace him as our shepherd, the Vicar of Christ, the Servant of the Servants of God.

Greg Erlandson
President
Our Sunday Visitor Publishing
April 27, 2005

INTRODUCTION

The idea for this book was first conceived several years ago during a conversation with Greg Erlandson, president and publisher of Our Sunday Visitor. We were discussing the flurry of activities that was likely to surround the passing of Pope John Paul II and the election of his successor. While aware even then of the magnitude of John Paul II — no one was prepared for the depth of emotion, the spiritual power, and the sheer historical significance of his funeral — we both realized clearly the amount of interest there would be in the next Pope to be chosen to follow in the footsteps of John Paul the Great.

It occurred to Greg that a biography, published immediately after the election of the new Pope, might go some way in introducing Our Sunday Visitor's readers to our new Pope.

From the start, we were determined that such a biography should not be merely a project crashed through the editorial process and rushed out into print to be number one. There will be several such books published over the next weeks and months. Nor is this book expected to be a final definitive biography of the new Vicar of Christ. Such a work must by its nature be the fruit of long reflection and undertaken after the shape and scope of the new pontificate can be assessed adequately. The very length of this book would preclude such ambitions and be impossible given the place of Joseph Ratzinger, now Benedict XVI, in the history of modern theology and contemporary Catholic affairs.

This book is intended to offer a first gentle introduction to the new Vicar of Christ, Successor to Peter, the Prince of the Apostles, and the Servant of the Servants of God. What we hope with this present volume is to provide readers with a sketch of sorts of the amazing events of the last weeks: the passing of Pope John Paul II as an eloquent icon of suffering conformed profoundly to Christ; the largest and most memorable funeral in Catholic history; the quiet but portentous days after John Paul's interment in St. Peter's Basilica; the ancient tradition of the conclave; and the triumphant declaration of the white smoke, the ringing of the bells, and Cardinal Medina Estevez's declaration, *"Habemus papam!"* From there, attention will be paid to the life of Pope Benedict XVI, who is now our shepherd. Throughout, readers will find excerpts from his brilliant writings and accounts of the events that shaped his life.

The last chapter of this book is devoted to assessing the challenges, crises, and opportunities confronting Pope Benedict XVI, with an eye toward forecasting what he might do in dealing with them. We do not know what kind of a Pope he will be or what he has in store for all of us who still mourn the passing of our beloved Karol Wojtyla.

And so a new pontificate commences, the 265th in the 2,000-year history of the Church. Papal history gives us little to go on for direction in anticipating what the next years will bring. Pope Benedict XVI is a pontiff acutely aware of the place of Pope John Paul II — who is likely in the future to be declared John Paul the Great, perhaps a saint, and maybe even a Doctor of the Church. The burdens of the papacy are heavy indeed, and the Shoes of the Fisherman are difficult to fill for any one Pope. Pope Benedict XVI begins his pontificate with a double challenge. Not only has he been asked to succeed to the Holy See and so inherit the challenges of his 264 predecessors, he is a new Pope following one of history's truly transcendent figures.

In assuming his place as successor to John Paul II and also to Saint Peter and all of the Popes between them, Joseph Ratzinger — as Benedict XVI — offers a chance to see the faith alive within the context of continuity and consolidation: Continuity in the decision of the College of Cardinals to provide certitude to the continuation of John Paul's own grand vision for the Church in a new millennium and consolidation in advancing further that vision in dialogue with a deeply troubled and conflicted world.

There is no question that Joseph Ratzinger was the best known, most famous, and most influential member of the College of Cardinals. He was the most towering figure entering a conclave since 1939 when Eugenio Pacelli entered as Secretary of State and Cardinal *Camerlengo*, along with a sparkling reputation for his diplomatic and intellectual gifts. Joseph Ratzinger emerged from the conclave in 2005 as Supreme Pontiff for many of the same reasons that Pacelli walked out of his in 1939 as Pope Pius XII. In its collective wisdom, guided by the Holy Spirit, the Sacred College concluded in four ballots over two days that he was ideally suited to carry forward the legacy of John Paul II in continuity and consolidation while remaining firmly and eloquently faithful to his own gifts and his authentic commitment to the Catholic faith.

His prominence and commanding presence in contemporary ecclesiastical affairs has been demonstrated in these first weeks by the inadvertent use of his name — Cardinal Joseph Ratzinger — instead of his adopted name as pontiff. This is not a sign of disrespect to our new Holy Father but is statement of how familiar we have all been with his theological writings, his works as Prefect of the Congregation for the Doctrine of the Faith, and his abiding role as a key advisor to John Paul II throughout the previous pontificate.

The challenges he faces are daunting, but Benedict XVI has long been preparing for this moment. He did not choose to be Pope. Indeed, he did not even wish to remain in the positions of power he had been given by the man he succeeds. Then Cardinal Ratzinger tried to leave as prefect of the Congregation of the Doctrine of the Faith in the early 1990's. But John Paul II, his friend and Pope, asked him to remain a laborer in the vineyard. And so he stayed. Now, at the age of 78, the oldest pontiff in nearly three centuries at the time of his election (older even than Blessed John XXIII at the time of his election in 1958), Joseph Ratzinger has one more task to accomplish. He must undertake one more labor in the vineyard. This time he has been asked by his fellow Cardinals. More importantly, he has been asked by the Holy Spirit, the same Spirit who called him to serve as a priest, who set him aside to be a Bishop and a Cardinal, and who has guided every step of his life as a follower of Christ.

While his pontificate may prove long or short, great or transitional, Pope Benedict XVI has been chosen for this role by his fellow Cardinals. Above all, he has been chosen by the Holy Spirit. That truth alone should bring hope and confidence.

Matthew E. Bunson, D.Min.
April 27, 2005

POPE BENEDICT XVI IN WORLD HISTORY

─────✠─────

A Chronology of Events

1922

Death of Pope Benedict XV. Pius XI becomes Pope.

1927

✠ April 16, Joseph Aloysius Ratzinger is born to Joseph and Mary Ratzinger in Marktl am Inn, Bavaria, Germany, on Holy Saturday and the Feast of St. Benedict Joseph Labré.

May 1, Adolf Hitler holds the first Nazi meeting in Berlin.

October 1, The Feast of St. Thérèse of Lisieux is made obligatory for the entire church.

1928

St. Josemaría Escrivá de Balaguer founds the future personal prelature Opus Dei in Spain.

March 5, Hitler's National Socialists win the majority vote in Bavaria, Joseph's home.

1929

✠ The Ratzinger family moves to Tittmoning, a small town on the Salzach River, on the Austrian border.

The Lateran Treaty creates the State of Vatican City.

1930

September 14, Nazis take 107 seats in German elections.

1931

December 7, a report indicates that Nazis would ensure "Nordic dominance" by sterilizing certain races.

1932

February 22, Adolf Hitler is the Nazi Party candidate for the presidential elections.

February 25, Adolf Hitler of Austria receives German citizenship

✠ December, Because of his outspoken criticism of the Nazis, Joseph Ratzinger moves his family again, this time to the small Alpine town of Aschau am Inn.

1933

January 30, German President Paul von Hindenburg makes Adolf Hitler chancellor.

February 19, Herman Göring, Nazi Prussian minister, bans all Catholic newspapers.

February 22, Nazi Herman Göring forms the secret police force.

March 31, German Republic gives dictatorial power to Hitler.

June 13, The Gestapo (Secret Police) is established.

December 23, Pope Pius XI condemns the Nazi sterilization program.

1934

The first Image of Divine Mercy is painted by E. Kazimierowski in Vilnius.

June 30, Adolf Hitler begins his "blood purge" of political and military leaders.

1935

November 14, Nazis strip German Jews of their citizenship.

November 28, The German Reich declares all men ages 18 to 45 to be army reservists.

1936

February 11, The Reich arrests 150 Catholic youth leaders in Berlin.

August 1, The 11th Olympic Games, dubbed "The Nazi Games," opens in Berlin.

November 15, Nazi Germany and Japan sign the Anti-Komintern pact.

1937

March, the encyclical *Mit Brennender Sorge* ("With Burning Sorrow") is smuggled into Germany. Cardinal Eugenio Pacelli (later Pius XII) helped Pius XI draft the work, which denounced Nazi paganism and racism.

Leftists in Spain disestablish the Church there.

✠ The elder Joseph Ratzinger retires from the police forces and moves his family to Hufschlag, outside the city of Traunstein. Young Joseph spent most of his teenage years here and studied classics and classical languages at the local gymnasium.

1938

April 10, Germany annexes Austria.

July 22, The Third Reich issues special identity cards for Jewish Germans.

1939

February 10, Pope Pius XI dies.

March 2, Pius XII becomes Pope.

April 5, Membership in Hitler Youth becomes obligatory.

May 22, Adolf Hitler and Benito Mussolini sign a "Pact of Steel" forming the Axis powers.

September 1, 4:40 a.m., World War II begins.

September 3, Britain and France declare war on Germany, two days after the Nazi invasion of Poland.

September 6, the first German air attack on Great Britain.

September 27, Germany occupies Warsaw.

October 6, Hitler announces plans to resolve "the Jewish problem."

✠ Young Joseph Ratzinger enters the minor seminary in Traunstein, beginning his preparation for ordination to the priesthood.

1940

Pope Pius XII announces that the Catholic Church will remain strictly neutral in the War.

June 4, German forces enter Paris.

June 10, Italy enters WWII.

Japan officially enters WWII.

June 14, the first inmates arrive at Auschwitz.

July 23, German bombers begin the "Blitz," the all-night air raids on London.

1941

✠ Joseph Ratzinger, age 14, is forced to join the Hitler Youth.

August 15, Martyrdom of St. Maximilian Kolbe in Dachau concentration camp.

August 22, German troops reach Leningrad.

October 25, German troops attack Moscow.

December 7, Bombing of Pearl Harbor by Japan; the United States enters WWII.

1942

January 20, Top Nazis formulate the "Final Solution" to the Jewish question.

June 4-7, Japan is defeated at the Battle of Midway, a turning point in the war.

August 9, Carmelite nun St. Teresa Benedicta of the Cross, born Edith Stein in 1891, is executed at Auschwitz

1943

✠ Joseph Ratzinger, along with many of his classmates, is drafted into the German army anti-aircraft corps.

April 29, Lutheran theologian Dietrich Bonhoeffer is arrested by Nazis; he is executed in 1945 by the Gestapo.

June 19, Rome bombed for first time.

June 10, The Allies begin round-the-clock bombing of Germany.

July 12, Pope Pius XII receives Baron von Weizsacker, the German ambassador.

September 10, German troops occupy Rome

1944

June 3, Nazis pull out of Rome.

June 6, D-Day, marking the effort to liberate France and Western Europe from Nazi Occupation

✠ September 10, Ratzinger and his class released from the corps.

✠ September, Ratzinger receives new draft notice and is posted to the Hungarian border area of Austria where he sets up anti-tank defenses.

✠ November 20, Ratzinger's unit is released from service.

1945

January 26, Soviet forces liberate Auschwitz.

February 3, The Allies drop 3,000 tons of bombs on Berlin.

March 12, Anne Frank, author of *The Diary of Anne Frank*, dies at Bergen-Belsen concentration camp a month before it is liberated.

April 30, Adolf Hitler commits suicide.

✠ May, Ratzinger deserts the army and returns home. He is then briefly interned in an open-air prisoner-of-war camp near Ulm.

✠ June 19, Ratzinger is released and returns home.

August 6, the United States drops the first Atomic Bomb on Hiroshima.

September 2, Japan surrenders, ending WWII.

✠ November, Joseph and his brother Georg re-enter the seminary.

1946-1951

✠ Ratzinger studies philosophy and theology at the University of Munich and at the higher school in Freising.

1948

June 24, The Berlin airlift begins.

November 30, Communists complete the division of Berlin, installing the government in the Soviet sector.

1950

November 1, Dogma of the Assumption of Mary is proclaimed by Pope Pius XII.

1951

✠ June 29, Georg and Joseph Ratzinger are ordained priests by Cardinal von Faulhaber, in the Cathedral at Freising, on the Feast of Sts. Peter and Paul. Joseph spends a year in pastoral ministry.

1953

✠ July, Father Joseph Ratzinger receives a doctorate in theology. His doctoral thesis is entitled *Volk und Haus Gottes in Augustins Lehre von der Kirche* ("The People and House of God in St. Augustine's Doctrine of the Church").

1955

May 5, West Germany becomes a sovereign state.

1957

✠ Father Ratzinger completes his Habilitation — a book-length effort at original research to receive permission to teach at the university level. He chooses Bonaventure's theology of history and revelation.

1958

October 9, Pope Pius XII dies.
October 28 Pope John XXIII is elected

1959

✠ April 15, Ratzinger starts as a full professor of fundamental theology at the University of Bonn.
✠ August 23, Joseph Ratzinger's father passes away after suffering a stroke.

1961

August 31, The Berlin Wall is erected.

1962-1965

October 11, 1962, Start of the Second Vatican Council.

✠ Ratzinger serves as a theological advisor (or *peritus*) to the Archbishop of Cologne, Cardinal Joseph Frings, at Vatican Council II.

1963

June 3, Pope John XIII dies.

June 21, Pope Paul VI is elected.

✠ Father Ratzinger moves to the University of Münster.

✠ December 16, Father Ratzinger's mother passes away.

1966

✠ Father Ratzinger accepts a second chair in dogmatic theology at the University of Tübingen.

1968

✠ The University of Tübingen is rocked by the student uprisings that troubled Europe and the United States. Father Ratzinger is deeply disturbed by the proliferation of Marxist political ideology among the students and professors, including within the theology department.

1969

✠ Father Ratzinger accepts a chair in theology and the history of dogma at the University of Regensburg; he later becomes dean and vice president and eventually theological advisor to the German bishops.

✠ Father Ratzinger is appointed to the International Theological Commission.

1972

August 26, the summer Olympic games open in Munich, West Germany.

✠ Father Ratzinger, along with such luminaries as Hans Urs von Balthasar and Henri de Lubac, helps to launch the Catholic theological journal *Communio*.

1977

✠ March 24, Pope Paul VI names Father Ratzinger Archbishop of Munich-Freising.

✠ June 27, Pope Paul VI elevates Archbishop Ratzinger to the College of Cardinals.

1978

August 6, Pope Paul VI dies.

August 26, Pope John Paul I elected.

September 28, Pope John Paul I dies.

October 16, Pope John Paul II elected

Mother Teresa of Calcutta receives Nobel Peace Prize

1980

✠ Cardinal Ratzinger is named relator of the 5th General Assembly of the Synod of Bishops by Pope John Paul II. Soon after, the Pope asks him to head the Congregation for Catholic Education. Ratzinger declines owing to his brief time as Archbishop of Munich-Freising.

1981

May 13, Assassination attempt on Pope John Paul II

✠ November 25, Pope John Paul II calls Ratzinger to Rome to be prefect of the Congregation for the Doctrine of the Faith, which is responsible for enforcing church orthodoxy. He is also named president of the Biblical Commission and of the Pontifical International Theological Commission.

1982

August 23, Opus Dei becomes the personal Prelature of the Pope.

October 10, Maximillian Kolbe is beatified.

1983

✠ Ratzinger becomes president delegate to the sixth Synodal Assembly.

1984

Diplomatic relations established between the Vatican and the U.S.

1985

Formal treaty between the Vatican and Italy replaces the Lateran Treaty of 1929.

1986-1992

✠ Ratzinger serves as president of the Commission for the Preparation of the Catechism of the Catholic Church.

1989

November 9, The Berlin Wall comes down and Germany is reunited after four decades of political division.

The Revised Code of Canon Law is promulgated.

1990

September 20, East and West Germany reunite officially.

1991

✠ Cardinal Ratzinger's elder sister Maria dies.

✠ September, Ratzinger suffers a cerebral hemorrage.

1993

Pope John Paul II issues the encyclical *Veritatis Splendor* ("The Splendor of the Truth").

✠ April 5, Ratzinger is elevated to the rank of Cardinal Bishop and named to the suburbicarian see of Velletri-Segni.

1994

The Catechism of the Catholic Church is issued in the United States

1995

Pope John Paul II issues the encyclical *Evangelium Vitae* ("The Gospel of Life").

1997

October 1, Pope John Paul II names St. Thérèse of Lisieux a Doctor of the Church.

1998

✠ November 6, Ratzinger is elected vice-dean of the College of Cardinals.

1999

October 31, Leaders of the Roman Catholic and modern Lutheran Churches in Germany sign the Augsburg Accord, a "Joint Declaration on the Doctrine of Justification."

2000

Pope John Paul II celebrates the Jubilee.

✠ The Vatican releases the famous "Third Secret" of Fatima; Cardinal Ratzinger writes a meditation on the secret.

August 6, Pope John Paul II approves the publication of *Dominus Iesus* ("Declaration on the Unicity and Salvific Universality of Jesus Christ and the Church").

2001

September 11, Terrorist attack on the United States of America.

2002

✠ November 30, Cardinal Ratzinger is elected dean of the College of Cardinals and so receives also the title of the suburbicarian see of Ostia.

2005

April 2, Pope John Paul II dies.

✠ April 8, As Dean of the College of Cardinals, Cardinal Ratzinger is the chief celebrant and homilist at the funeral mass for Pope John Paul II.

✠ April 19, The College of Cardinals elects Joseph Ratzinger as the 264th successor to St. Peter. He takes the name Benedict XVI.

PART I

Sede Vacante: The Vacant See

Chapter 1

FAREWELL TO A BELOVED POPE

———✠———

We can be sure that our beloved Pope is standing today at the window of the Father's house, that he sees us and blesses us. Yes, bless us, Holy Father. We entrust your dear soul to the Mother of God, your Mother, who guided you each day and who will guide you now to the eternal glory of her Son, our Lord Jesus Christ. Amen.

— CARDINAL JOSEPH RATZINGER,
HOMILY, FUNERAL OF POPE JOHN PAUL II

On the chilly evening of April 2, 2005, over sixty thousand Catholics and non-Catholics, Italians and foreign pilgrims, and hundreds of members of the international media gathered in St. Peter's Square to pray for the health and the safe final journey of the pontiff they had come to know and to love over the last twenty-seven years. As the crowd took part in reciting the rosary, however, Archbishop Leonardo Sandri, *sostituto*, or substitute, of the Vatican Secretariat of State, walked to the microphone positioned on the steps of the basilica. He declared in Italian, "At 9:37 p.m., our Holy Father returned to the House of the Father." Pope John Paul II was dead. The 26-year pontificate of one of the greatest Popes had drawn to a close.

Even though the death had been anticipated and even expected, grief struck like a shock wave across the crowd and the world. In an irony of the modern age of communications, viewers of television networks around the planet knew that the Pope had entered what Archbishop Giovanni Comastri, vicar general for the Vatican City State, called "the doors opened by Christ"before the crowds in the square. The press had been informed immediately in what proved the first of many innovations. With the certification of death, the Holy See Press Office sent out a wave of e-mails.

At last, in a centuries-old custom, a single bell tolled in the tower of St. Peter's Basilica. The clarion sound of the lone bell was soon joined by other ringing as bells across the city of Rome sounded out. Soon, bells pealed out across the globe as the Catholic Church's one billion members learned of the pontiff's passing and paused to pray, reflect, and mourn the end of an era.

The *Camerlengo's* Duty

Even before the bells had been rung, the Cardinal *Camerlengo* (the papal chamberlain), the Spaniard Eduardo Cardinal Martinez Somalo, had completed the ceremonial tasks of making certain that Pope John Paul II had, in fact, died. The old custom of using a silver hammer to tap the deceased Pope three times on the forehead was discontinued some decades ago. But the accompanying practice of calling out the Pope's Christian name three times was retained. Cardinal Martinez Somalo did not receive any response to his cries of "Karol!" and concurred with the conclusion of the doctors that John Paul was truly gone.

Once the certification was complete, Cardinal Somalo officially informed Cardinal Camillo Ruini, Vicar of the Diocese of Rome. Soon after, messages were dispatched by Cardinal Joseph Ratzinger, dean of the College of Cardinals, to his fellow members of the Sacred College of Cardinals. The missive was no doubt short, for the Cardinals in Rome could be certain that their fellow members of the College were already on their way to Rome. The last time a Cardinal *Camerlengo* had sent out such announcements — in 1978 — the Church official, the French Cardinal and Secretary of State Jean Villot, had sent a simple but firm notice: "POPE DEAD, COME QUICKLY."

Once the telegrams were gone to the Cardinal Electors of 52 countries (those under the age of 80), Somalo launched into the program that had long been prepared. The Catholic Church was now officially in the grim but expectant period of the *sede vacante* — the vacant see. The diocese of Rome was without a bishop, and thus the Church was without a pontiff. All formal activities and proceedings of the Church's central government in Rome ceased, and virtually every key office holder, such as the prefects and pro-prefects of the congregations, councils, and committees of the Curia, ceased to have jobs, save for a few key personnel. The exceptions were the *Camerlengo* whose job was to oversee the upcoming conclave; the Vicar of Rome, Cardinal Camillo Ruini, as day-to-day administration was still essential in the diocese of Rome; and the Major Penitentiary, the American Cardinal James Stafford, whose task was to ensure that the sacrament of penance is available for all Christians regardless of the presence of the Pope.

The Passing of the Pontiff

Clearly declining in health over the previous months, the Pope had been taken to Gemelli Hospital near the Vatican on January 30 (the same hospital where his life had been hanging by a thread in 1981 after the assassination attempt by Mehmet Ali Agca, and where he had been hospitalized several times from ailments and illnesses). His last days were marked by continuing deterioration, another trip to Gemelli, and a return to the Vatican in time for Holy Week celebrations culminating with his appearances on Easter Sunday and finally on Wednesday of the Octave of Easter.

On these final occasions, the pontiff had tried to speak but could manage only a few whispered sounds before giving up in futility. He gave a feeble blessing — a transfixing moment that highlighted the image he had borne for the last years as an icon of suffering and as one who had conformed his immense sufferings to those of Christ. By Thursday evening, the Vatican was announcing that the Holy Father had entered into what were almost certainly his final hours. By Friday evening, Italian news agencies and even one American cable news channel had declared his death prematurely. The next evening, the reports of his death were true.

The death of John Paul II achieved yet another of his surprises that had become one of the greatest hallmarks of his twenty-six-year pontificate. Within hours of the bells tolling in St. Peter's and Rome, pilgrims, faithful, and people from all over the world were heading to Rome in a flood of humanity that overshadowed the far quieter journey to Rome by the Cardinals.

Though spread out across the globe, the Cardinals reacted to the news with a nearly universal emphasis on the legacy of John Paul II and an abiding awareness of their own sacred duty that had been thrust upon them. Cardinal Julius Darmaatmadja, S.J., Archbishop of Jakarta, Indonesia, spoke to the media briefly before setting out for Rome with Indonesian President Susilo Bambang Yudhoyono, using the moment to instruct his countrymen on the purpose and value of a conclave. He said, for example, "History proves that the one elected as a Pope is the one elected by God," and reminded the reporters that while there were to be 117 Cardinals taking part, each one responds in his own way to the promptings of the Holy Spirit, hears a "secret voice," and names the Cardinal who is truly deserving to be placed in charge of the Holy See.

Cardinal George Pell, Archbishop of Sydney, Australia, commented: "What we have lost is a man who was universally recognized as not only the best known but the most effective preacher and teacher of Christ in the world, and one of the most extraordinary Popes in the history of the Church. He will be known as John Paul the Great." Cardinal Cormac-Murphy O'Connor said before heading for Rome, "Naturally like everyone else in the Catholic Church, we feel sad and, in a way, orphaned by the death of Pope John Paul . . . There's so much one could say about Pope John Paul and what is interesting is that all over the word people are recalling what he said and did. Above all, it's the memory of a quite unique and remarkable man whom the good

> *He will be known as John Paul the Great.*
>
> — CARDINAL GEORGE PELL

Lord gave us as Pope for a long time and whose memory will always be treasured."

Meanwhile, Catholics and non-Catholics, the rich and the poor, men and women of every nationality and color, families and single people, the young and the old, made their way to Rome in a sight that was more reminiscent of the grand pilgrimages of faith of the Middle Ages than a modern trip to the Italian capital. They came quite literally by the millions to see him, to share in the grief, the bittersweet funeral that would celebrate his entry into a new life, and to honor him one last time for the refrain heard by over one billion people in 104 trips across the globe: *Totus Tuus* ("All for You").

By Monday, April 4, as the Pope lay in state in the Sala Clementina in the Apostolic Palace, people were already camped out in St. Peter's Basilica to be first in line to see the Holy Father when he was brought into the Basilica. The following morning, the first public procession of the *sede vacante* was held when the body — dressed in red-and-gold vestments, crowned with a white miter, the shepherd's staff tucked beneath his left arm, and a rosary wrapped in his folded hands — was carried solemnly from the Apostolic Palace, into the Square and into the Basilica.

By Tuesday morning, there were over 65 Cardinals in Rome, and those who could took part in the procession. The symbolism was unmistakable. The Cardinals, striking in their scarlet choir dress, led the procession. Visually, the world was being told that the Pope was truly dead and the caretakers of the Church were present. They walked somberly, followed by the Cardinal *Camerlengo*, Cardinal Martinez Somalo, and then the deceased Pope's body. The bier was carried by a group of ushers who had served the papal Masses and were called Gentlemen of His Holiness, flanked by members of the Swiss Guard and monks from the Eternal City's many monastic houses.

But the loss of the Pope was still too sharp, and the formal procession was greeted in the Square by the gasps of the faithful, applause in the Italian tradition to salute the dead, and calls of praise and honor for the dead pontiff. As the Gentlemen reached the threshold of the Basilica, they turned the bier to display John Paul's face one final time to the multitude. Exhausted from his long days since the papal death, the 78-year-old Cardinal Martinez Somalo choked back tears at that moment for his friend and his boss of over two decades.

A Funeral for the Ages

And then they started to arrive, by the thousands, the hundreds of thousands, and then the millions. The line of people waiting to see the pontiff as he rested on a catafalque near the main altar stretched from the Basilica, along a zigzagging line across the piazza, down the Via della Conciliazione, past Castel Sant'Angelo, and over the Tiber. They waited for eighteen hours for the briefest of glimpses. They said a prayer, shed a tear, said farewell, and were forced to move on to make way for the next person in line eager to see him. The endless line was marked by its eerie silences, the calm of the people, the friendliness of the participants, and above all the multitude of faces and languages on display. Some ten thousand volunteers assisted in the care of pilgrims and handed out three million free bottles of water. Twenty-one medical posts were also established to provide first aid to the many who fainted from heat and congestion.

They kept coming right up until the last possible moment when the doors to St. Peter's were closed and the *Sampietrini*, the workers of the Basilica, had to make ready for the funeral. If the lines had given assurance of anything, it was that the mourning was not soon to end and that John Paul II had still more surprises in store for the Church and the world.

On April 8, at ten in the morning Rome time, Cardinal Joseph Ratzinger, 164 members of the College of Cardinals, and the patriarchs of the Eastern Catholic Churches gathered for the funeral Mass for the Pope. What had been planned as a traditional obsequy for a pontiff had escalated very quickly into, quite literally, the largest funeral in human history.

In attendance were representatives from 169 countries, including 10 monarchs, 59 heads of state, 3 heirs to the throne, 17 heads of government, 8 vice heads of state, 6 deputy prime ministers, 4 presidents of parliaments, 24 ambassadors, and 10 presidents, directors-general, and secretaries-general of international organizations. The Orthodox Churches were represented by 23 delegations, and there were 8 other churches and ecclesial communions from the Western Hemisphere as well as representatives from three international Christian organizations. Further, there were several official delegations of Judaism and seventeen delegations from non-Christian religions and various organizations dedicated to interreligious dialogue.

As he had in life, John Paul had brought the bitterest of enemies together, united at least for the moment in their common agreement on the honors due him. At the Sign of Peace during the Mass, the representatives of Israel shook hands with their counterparts from Iran and Syria. While they later assured the press that the gestures were hardly meaningful statements of future peace, they were a reminder of the dead Pope's comment when criticized that he should not be talking to the Palestinians, "It is hard to make peace with someone you are not talking to."

> *Pope John Paul II was, himself, an inspiration to millions of Americans, and to so many more throughout the world. We will always remember the humble, wise and fearless priest who became one of history's great moral leaders.*
>
> — GEORGE W. BUSH, PRESIDENT OF THE UNITED STATES OF AMERICA

Some 500,000 people packed St. Peter's Square and the Via della Conciliazione. As a reporter for *USA Today* wrote, however, the entire city of Rome had become a church. Large television screens were installed across the city to encourage people to watch from other locations besides St. Peter's. So, 600,000 people watched the Mass on 28 giant screens placed throughout Rome, including at the two football stadiums, Tor Vergata University, the Circus Maximus, the basilicas of St. John Lateran, St. Mary Major, and St. Paul's Outside-the-Walls, the Piazza del Popolo, the Piazza Risorgimento, and the Colosseum. Estimates placed the attendance at four million, effectively doubling the population of the Eternal City for the event.

In the Square, the simple cypress coffin bearing the remains of John Paul II was placed upon an ornate carpet on the floor of the piazza. A copy of the Gospels was placed atop the coffin, and an Easter candle was lit nearby. As the Mass went on, a strong breeze turned the pages of the open book back and forth in a moment eerily reminiscent of the funeral of Pope Paul VI in 1978. There, on a gloomy day in August, the Gospel book had also been ruffled. Here, finally, the book was closed to prevent the pages from being torn out completely.

Cardinal Ratzinger delivered the homily. Speaking for the entire Church, but also speaking as one who had known Karol Wojtyla for decades and who called him friend, he said:

> "Follow me." The Risen Lord says these words to Peter. They are his last words to this disciple, chosen to shepherd his flock. "Follow me" — this lapidary saying of Christ can be taken as the key to understanding the message which comes to us from the life of our late beloved Pope John Paul II. Today we bury his remains in the earth as a seed of immortality — our hearts are full of sadness, yet at the same time of joyful hope and profound gratitude. These are the sentiments that inspire us, Brothers and Sisters in Christ, present here in Saint Peter's Square, in neighboring streets, and in various other locations within the city of Rome, where an immense crowd, silently praying, has gathered over the last few days . . .
>
> The Holy Father was a priest to the last, for he offered his life to God for his flock and for the entire human family, in a daily self-oblation for the service of the Church, especially amid the sufferings of his final months. And in this way he became one with Christ, the Good Shepherd who loves his sheep. Finally, "abide in my love": the Pope who tried to meet every-

one, who had an ability to forgive and to open his heart to all, tells us once again today, with these words of the Lord, that by abiding in the love of Christ we learn, at the school of Christ, the art of true love . . .

Our Pope — and we all know this — never wanted to make his own life secure, to keep it for himself; he wanted to give of himself unreservedly, to the very last moment, for Christ and thus also for us. And thus he came to experience how every-thing which he had given over into the Lord's hands came back to him in a new way. His love of words, of poetry, of literature, became an essential part of his pastoral mission and gave new vitality, new urgency, new attractiveness to the preaching of the Gospel, even when it is a sign of contradiction . . .

He heard the words of the crucified Lord as addressed per-sonally to him: "Behold your Mother." And so he did as the beloved disciple did: he took her "into his own home" (Jn. 19:27) — *Totus tuus*. And from the mother he learned to con-form himself to Christ.

None of us can ever forget how on that last Easter Sunday of his life, the Holy Father, marked by suffering, came once more to the window of the Apostolic Palace and one last time gave his blessing *urbi et orbi*. We can be sure that our beloved Pope is standing today at the window of the Father's house, that he sees us and blesses us. Yes, bless us, Holy Father. We entrust your dear soul to the Mother of God, your Mother, who guided you each day and who will guide you now to the eternal glory of her Son, our Lord Jesus Christ. Amen.

As with those taking part via television around Rome, the vast throng in the Square knelt at the appropriate times and took part in all of the prayers. The emotion of the moment, though, was uncon-trollable, and spontaneous applause periodically erupted, climaxing in the cathartic moments at the end of the Mass. As the commenda-tion of the body was begun by Cardinal Camillo Ruini, cries of *"Magnus! Magnus!"* rang out in the cool Roman air by the thousands, demanding that John Paul be recognized as "the Great," an honor bestowed on only three previous pontiffs, Gregory I, Leo I, and Nicholas (although his title is less widely recognized). Such a scene had not been witnessed in Rome since 604 and Gregory's own funeral when chants were made in identical fashion: *"Magnus! Magnus!"* Still others cried out for the immediate canonization of John Paul II. They were especially loud as Cardinal Ratzinger finished his homily, accompanied by sustained applause. Banners were waving in the wind with the words, *Santo Subito* ("saint immediately") and thousands waved white handkerchiefs.

The Mass ended with a prayer of commendation by Cardinal Ruini, and then with an unprecedented patriarchal prayer by the leadership of the Eastern Catholic Churches from around the world. A solemn chant brought the huge crowd to utter silence as the patriarchs sang their own prayers of farewell, including the *Kyrie Eleison*. With final prayers, the coffin was lifted by the Gentlemen of His Holiness and brought back into St. Peter's Basilica. As they had done on Tuesday, the Gentlemen stopped at the threshold of the basilica and turned the coffin to face the crowd. The faithful cheered one final time, and the body of Pope John Paul II was carried into the shadows of the church he had called his own, and disappeared into the darkness within. In a moment that reiterated the relative statures of the pontiff and those who had come to mourn him, the most powerful leaders on earth made their way on foot as an informal group into the basilica after him.

The Final Farewell

His body was taken down into the Vatican Grottoes to the place that had been prepared for it. In 2000, Pope John XXIII was taken from his tomb in the Grottoes — a tomb at which Pope John Paul II had prayed — and installed beneath an altar in the basilica. This was due to his beatification by John Paul II in October of that year as well as to the fact that the Grottoes were too confined a space for the thousands who came to visit him. Now, the empty place created by Pope John XXIII's departure was filled with the coffin of one of his great successors, Pope John Paul II.

The ceremony of interment was attended by the *Camerlengo*, the Vicar of Rome, and the members of the Papal Household, including Archbishop Dziwisz. The cypress coffin was installed in a zinc casket and sealed by a torch. This was then situated within a finer wooden coffin of elm, a wood befitting the Supreme Pontiff. All three were then lowered into the ground and covered over with a simple stone slab with the words, "Ioannes Paulus II, P.P. 1920-2005." Below them on the slab was carved the ancient symbol of the Christian faith, the *chi-rho*, a P superimposed upon an X.

Prior to the funeral Mass, another private ceremony had been conducted in St. Peter's Basilica. The body of the Pope had been moved from the catafalque and placed into the cypress coffin. With it went a collection of papal coins, in different denominations, for each year of his pontificate, and the *Rogito*, the proclamation summarizing the life of Pope John Paul II. The document was read in its original Latin by Archbishop Piero Marini, the long-time Master of Papal Liturgical Ceremonies, and was then placed in the coffin encased in a metal tube to preserve it for all time. (See the text of the *Rogito* on pages 44-46.)

On April 12, Vatican spokesman Joaquín Navarro-Valls gave a final report on the staggering numbers involving the funeral and its emotional week. Three million people had journeyed to Rome to attend the funeral. The funeral itself was covered by over 6,000 members of the media, including journalists, photographers, and radio and television reporters; some 137 television networks from over 80 countries had informed the Pontifical Council for Social Communications that they would be broadcasting the funeral Mass, although the general belief was that many other countries also broadcast the event or it was seen by their citizens.

The Rogito

In the light of the Risen Christ, the 2nd of April in the year of the Lord 2005, at 21:37 in the evening, while it turned toward the end of Saturday, and having already entered into the Lord's Day, the Octave of Easter and Divine Mercy Sunday, the beloved Pastor of the Church John Paul II passed from this world to the Father. The entire Church, especially the youth, has accompanied his passage in prayer.

John Paul II was the 264th Pope. His memory remains in the heart of the Church and the entirety of mankind.

Karol Wojtyla, elected Pope 16 October 1978, was born at Wadowice, a city 50 kilometers from Kraków, on 18 May 1920 and baptized two days later in the parish church by Fr. Francis Zak.

At age nine he received his first Holy Communion, at eighteen years the sacrament of confirmation. Interrupted in his studies because the Nazi army of occupation had closed the University, he worked in a quarry, and subsequently, in the Solvay chemical factory. At the end of 1942, sensing that he was called to the priesthood, he attended the course of formation of the clandestine seminary of Kraków. On 1 November 1946 he received priestly ordination by the hand of Cardinal Adam Sapieha. Then he was sent to Rome where he pursued the licentiate and doctorate in theology with the thesis entitled *Doctrina de fide apud Sanctum Ioannem a Cruce.*

He returned next to Poland, where there would be some pastoral ministry and the teaching of sacred discipline. On 4 July 1958 Pope Pius XII named him auxiliary bishop of Kraków, and by Paul VI, in 1964, he was destined to the same see as Archbishop. As such he intervened in the Second Vatican Council. Paul VI created him Cardinal 26 June 1967.

In the Conclave he was elected Pope by the Cardinals on 16 October 1978, and took the name John Paul II. On 22 October, the Lord's Day, he solemnly began his Petrine ministry.

The Pontificate of John Paul II has been one of the longest in Church history. In this period, under various aspects, many changes have been seen. Numbered among them was the fall of some regimes to which he himself contributed. For the purpose of announcing the Gospel, he completed many journeys in various nations.

John Paul II has exercised the Petrine ministry with a tireless missionary spirit, dedicating all his energy, urged on by solicitude for the entire Church and by a charity opened to the entirety of humanity. More than each predecessor, he has encounter the People of God and the responsible leaders of nations, in celebrations, in general and in special audiences and in pastoral visits.

In his love for youth he pushed to begin World Youth Days, calling together millions of young people in various parts of the world.

He successfully promoted dialogue with the Jewish people and with representatives of other religions, calling them together sometimes in an encounter of prayer for peace, especially in Assisi.

He has notably enlarged the College of Cardinals creating 231 (1 more *in pectore*). He has convoked 15 Assemblies of the Synod of Bishops, 7 general and 8 special. He has erected numerous dioceses and administrations, in particular in Eastern Europe.

He reformed the Western and Eastern Codes of Canon Law, created new institutions and reorganized the Roman Curia.

As "high priest" he exercised the liturgical ministry in the Diocese of Rome and throughout the globe, in full fidelity to the Second Vatican Council. He promoted, in an exemplary manner, life and liturgical spirituality and contemplative prayer, especially Eucharistic adoration and the prayer of the Holy Rosary (cfr. Ap. Let. *Rosarium Virginis Mariae*).

Under his guidance the Church has approached the third millennium and has celebrated the Great Jubilee of 2000, following the lines indicated with the apostolic letter *Tertio millennio adveniente*. She then entered into the new era, receiving indications in the apostolic letter *Novo millennio ineunte*, in which was shown to the faithful the way to the future.

With the Year of the Redemption , the Marian Year, and the Year of the Eucharist, he promoted the spiritual renewal of the Church. He gave an extraordinary impulse to canonizations and beatifications, in order to show innumerable examples of sanctity today, that it would be an inducement to men of our time. He proclaimed St. Thérèse of the Child Jesus a Doctor of the Church.

The doctrinal Magisterium of John Paul II is very rich. Custodian of the Deposit of the Faith, he did his best with wisdom and courage to promote Catholic doctrine, theological, moral, and spiritual, and to oppose during all of his pontificate tendencies contrary to the genuine tradition of the Church.

Among the principle documents are numbered 14 Encyclicals, 15 Apostolic Exhortations, 11 Apostolic Constitutions, 45 Apostolic Letters, in addition to Catecheses proposed in the general audiences and the allocutions delivered in every part of the world. With his teaching John Paul II has confirmed and illuminated the People of God on the theological doctrine (above all in the first three great Encyclicals — *Redemptor hominis, Dives in misericordia, Dominum et vivificantem*), anthropological and social (Encyclicals *Laborem exercens, Sollicitudo re socialis, Centesimus annus*), moral (Encyclicals *Veritatis splendor, Evangelium vitae*), ecumenical (Encyclical *Ut unum sint*), missiological (Encyclical *Redemptoris missio*), mariological (Encyclical *Redemptoris mater*).

He has promulgated the *Catechism of the Catholic Church*, in the light of Tradition, authoritatively interpreted by the Second Vatican Council. He also published some volumes as a private Doctor.

His Magisterium culminated in the Encyclical *Ecclesia de Eucharistia* and in the Apostolic Letter *Mane nobiscum Domine*.

John Paul II has left to all an admirable testimony of piety, of a holy life, and of universal fatherhood.

A Daunting Task

The Cardinals were gathered, and there now remained for them one more task. The Pope was dead, and the cries of *"Magnus! Magnus!"* by the crowd in St. Peter's Square and across the Church had made the mammoth labor of the Cardinals even weightier: to choose his successor.

In the days since the passing of Karol Wojtyla, the 264th Pope, what had been thought privately by many and said publicly by some had now been recognized by all. The influence and the spiritual majesty of Pope John Paul II the Great lived on.

Chapter 2

BETWEEN THE REIGNS
—————✠—————

Now is the time for silence and prayer.

— CARDINAL CHRISTOPH SCHÖNBORN

The Cardinals' Silence

A deceptive quiet descended on Rome in the days immediately after the funeral of Pope John Paul II. The vast majority of pilgrims and Catholics who had made their way to the Eternal City to witness the funeral Mass set out for home, unable to afford the cost of remaining in the city until the end of the conclave that was set to begin ten days later, on April 18. The American media, itself exhausted from a steady week of papal coverage, turned its attention to the nuptials of Prince Charles and Camilla Parker-Bowles on Saturday, April 9, and the more mundane squabbles of U.S. politics. Reports were still being made from the Vatican by journalists, but there was a noticeable decline in their length and intensity. There was a collective sense of recuperating after the week of farewell to John Paul.

Beneath this calm, however, there remained two inescapable realities. The first was that the 6,000 reporters in Rome still had to cover the second part of the two-act drama that is the *sede vacante*. While international attention was taken off of Rome, reporters — especially longtime Vatican watchers — were focusing their attentions on the subtle and nuanced process at work among the Cardinals. The articles that followed in the days immediately after the funeral centered, however, not on what the Cardinals might be thinking but on two ultimately peripheral events.

On Monday, April 11, American Cardinal Bernard Law said one of the Masses for the repose of the soul of John Paul II in the Basilica

of Santa Maria Maggiore. While his presence as celebrant was war-
ranted by his position as Archpriest of the Basilica, controversy
attended the Mass because of Law's resignation as Archbishop of
Boston in December 2002 over the sex-abuse scandal in his archdiocese. The American media pounced on the story, encouraged by the
protests of Americans who had traveled to Rome and were members
of the victims advocacy group, SNAP (Survivors Network of those
Abused by Priests), that tries to keep the issue of the sex-abuse scandal an on-going one in the public consciousness of the Church. The
group went on to issue a manifesto at a press conference in Rome that
declared as "morally unacceptable candidates for the papacy" five Cardinals for their statements during the sex abuse scandal. The five were:
Cardinal Oscar Rodríguez Maradiaga of Tegucigalpa, Honduras; Cardinal Norberto Rivera Carrera of Mexico City; Italian Cardinal Angelo
Sodano, Vatican Secretary of State; Colombian Cardinal Darío Castrillón Hoyos, prefect of the Congregation for Clergy; and Cardinal
Francisco Errázuriz Ossa of Santiago, Chile. Three of the names —
Rodríguez Maradiaga, Catrillón Hoyos, and Sodano — had all
appeared on various lists of papal contenders. The group expected
other Cardinal Electors to be aware of the statements and actions of
the five and so discouraged them from considering the group as papal
successors.

The second reality that proved to have a major impact on coverage was the decision of the Cardinals at one of the first General
Congregations to a unanimously accepted promise not to speak to
the media. The Cardinals subsequently remained faithful to the decision, which according to reports was prompted by the concerns of
Cardinals from the Third World that their fellow members from the
First World — in particular those of the United States and Western
Europe — were receiving the bulk of attention and thus might wield
an excessive amount of influence on the proceedings. Thus, the only
significant surprise to emerge in the next days was that two Cardinals
eligible to vote would not take part, Jaime Sin of the Philippines and
Adolfo Suárez Rivera of Mexico. Cardinal Sin was one of only three

electors not to have been named by Pope John Paul II, having been appointed by Pope Paul VI in 1976. His absence brought to only two the number of Electors not named by John Paul II — the others being Cardinal Joseph Ratzinger and the American William Baum.

The low point of sorts arrived on April 15 when the announcement was made that work was being completed on a new chimney for the Sistine Chapel, meaning that the chimney would be used for the smoke from the Sistine Chapel announcing the progress of the Cardinals in their voting. Dr. Navarro-Valls informed the press that tests would be conducted using yellow smoke to make sure the chimney was fully functional. The new chimney was part of the process of avoiding a repeat of the events in the conclave of October 1978 when grey smoke appeared out of the chimney leaving the gathered crowds in St. Peter's Square confused as to whether a Pope had actually been elected. For the new conclave, an improved chimney was installed, connected to a makeshift stove installed on the left side entrance of the Chapel in which would be burned the ballots used in the different voting sessions. Traditionally, the ballots were burned with dry or wet straw to produce a black or white smoke and so alert the outside world as to progress in deliberations. Chemicals were to be used in the 2005 conclave to assist in the certainty of the announcement, and a new signal was added as well — upon certification of the vote, white smoke would be used, but the bells of St. Peter's would also be rung. To add emphasis, Cardinal Camillo Ruini

> ✠
>
> *We should await our new Bishop and Pope in the light of this same Spirit. Let us not be pointlessly and too humanly curious to know beforehand who he will be.*
>
> *Let us prepare ourselves instead to welcome in prayer, trust, and love the one whom the Lord chooses to give us.*
>
> — CARDINAL CAMILLO RUINI, HOMILY

declared that the bells of the many churches of Rome would also ring out.

A large group of reporters dutifully set up in the Square and focused their cameras on the three workers putting the finishing touches on the chimney and then lingered on the completed brick structure perched atop the Chapel and latched down by secure cables. The moment was the Roman equivalent of watching paint dry.

Bereft of useful quotes, the scrutiny of the press shifted to two time-honored customs during the *sede vacante*: listening attentively to the slightest hints placed within homilies for the perspectives of Cardinals who might be presiding over one of the Masses of the *Novemdiales* and relying upon the gossip, trade-in rumor, and sheer speculation of Vaticanistas as they talked with those who were in the know, who knew someone who was in the know, or who simply pretended to be in the know.

The homilies soon proved carefully worded and faithful to honoring and remembering John Paul II. Cardinal Law's homily, delivered in Italian, was overshadowed by the protests. One interesting moment did arrive with the typically eloquent homily of Cardinal Ruini on April 10, during the Mass for the Pope in St. Peter's Basilica as part of the *Novemdiales*. Ruini touched briefly but significantly upon the state of the world and especially the need for the Church to reach out and shine the light of the Gospel into every dark corner. As Cardinal Ruini declared, he envisioned "a Church that is not folded in upon itself, not timid, not lacking in trust, a Church burning with the love of Christ for the salvation of all men."

Focus centered as well on the lists of so-called *papabili*, those Cardinals considered for various reasons to have a genuine chance of being elected. The lists are a permanent fixture of papal elections and speculation as to a possible next Pope. As early as 1993, when Pope John Paul II began to suffer a serious decline in health, the first names began surfacing. The *papabili* lists — generated chiefly by journalists basing their estimates upon discussions with Church officials and other journalists — varied considerably as the pontificate went on, especially as some of the Cardinals seen as likely prospects to succeed John Paul were actually outlived by the pontiff. By the start of the *sede vacante*, the papabili lists included as many as twenty names, a testament to the remarkable diversity of the Church, espe-

THE PAPABILI

There is a famous cliché regarding papal elections that a Cardinal who enters a conclave as a Pope comes out still a Cardinal, meaning that history has proven likely candidates do not win very often. History would seem to support this maxim, and one need look only at the last two conclaves, both in 1978, to see evidence. Cardinal Albino Luciani of Venice was not on any lists of so-called *papabili* (papal favorites) entering the conclave to elect a successor to Pope Paul VI, but he was swiftly chosen as Pope John Paul I. After his sudden death barely a month later, Cardinal Karol Wojtyla was likewise nowhere to be found among the *papabili*. He was soon elected as Pope John Paul II.

In the months and days before the conclave in April 2005, the lists of papabili included a varied group of Cardinals. Joseph Ratzinger was among those named as strong candidates. Also among them were:

Cardinal Francis Arinze
Prefect of the Congregation for Divine Worship and the Discipline of the Sacraments
Age: 72
A convert to Catholicism and the former Archbishop of Onitsha, Nigeria, Cardinal Arinze is the leading African Cardinal. He was baptized and encouraged to become a priest by Father Cyprian Tansi of Nigeria (who was beatified by Pope John Paul II in 1998). He is also a noted author and well-respected for his efforts at interreligious dialogue and has played a key role in the recent efforts to renew the liturgy.

Cardinal Jorge Mario Bergoglio, S.J.

Archbishop of Buenos Aires, Argentina

Age: 68

A soft-spoken, austere, and humble Jesuit, Cardinal Bergoglio has a reputation for dedication to social justice that is matched by his conservative outlook regarding Church doctrine and spirituality. His humility is striking to observers — he generally uses public transportation and cooks his own meals. He also has a formidable reputation within Argentina as a deeply spiritual leader respected by every political faction.

Cardinal Godfried Danneels

Archbishop of Mechelen-Brussels, Belgium

Age: 71

A leading candidate among more liberal members of the College, Cardinal Daneels is a former professor of liturgy at the Catholic University of Louvain and is noted for his pastoral skill. He faces two major obstacles: he suffered a heart attack in 1997 and is a Cardinal from a region that suffers from severe doctrinal upheaval. Still, he speaks eloquently about the state of contemporary culture and compares modern European life to ancient Rome and its obsession with "bread and circuses."

Cardinal Claudio Hummes, O.F.M.

Archbishop of São Paulo, Brazil

Age: 70

A Franciscan, Cardinal Hummes is pastor of the largest archdiocese in Brazil, with over six million Catholics. He arrived with a conservative reputation but soon established himself as a shepherd who defied labels. Well respected in Rome, he preached the 2002 Lenten Retreat for the papal household; at the same time he opposed Brazil's old military regime and has long fought for workers' rights. He once observed that the proclamation of the person of Jesus Christ "necessarily must lead to the exercise of charity and solidarity with the poor."

Cardinal Norberto Rivera Carrera

Archbishop of Mexico City, Mexico

Age: 62

Archbishop of one of the world's largest archdioceses with some seven million Catholics, Cardinal Rivera Carrera is considered theologically conservative and played a key role in Pope John Paul II's visits in 1999 and 2002, especially the latter, at which Juan Diego was declared a saint. He is also an outspoken critic of globalization and its impact on the Third World as well as corruption in Mexican politics. Cardinal Rivera Carrera enjoys close relations with the Legionaries of Christ, an influential congregation founded in Mexico in 1941.

Cardinal Oscar Andrés Rodríguez Maradiaga, S.D.B.

Archbishop of Tegucigalpa, Honduras

Age: 62

A young and dynamic Cardinal, Rodriguez Maradiaga has three doctorates. He raised some eyebrows in recent years for his defense of then Boston Cardinal Bernard Law during the Church's sexual abuse scandal and his determined call for debt relief for the Third World. He is a member of the Salesians and is well-known in Latin America through his service as president of the CELAM (the Latin American Bishops' Conference) from 1995-1999. He also plays the piano, can pilot his own airplane, and speaks multiple languages.

Cardinal Christoph Schönborn, O.P.

Archbishop of Vienna

Age: 60

A Dominican and a member of an ancient Austrian noble family, Cardinal Schönborn served as general editor of the *Catechism of the Catholic Church* and is a well-respected theologian and former student of Cardinal Joseph Ratzinger. He became Archbishop of Vienna in 1995 after the resignation of his predecessor for sexual impropriety and has labored to bring healing among the faithful in the face of the sexual scandal of recent years. He has also promoted evangelization in Eastern Europe still recovering from Communist atheism.

Cardinal Angelo Scola

Patriarch of Venice

Age: 63

A leading conservative theologian in Italy and the respected former rector of the Pontifical Lateran University in Rome, Cardinal Scola has astonished Venice and northern Italy with his energy and pastoral zeal. The son of a truck driver, he went on to become a close collaborator with the great theologians Henri de Lubac and Hans Urs von Balthasar. He is a supporter of lay ecclesial movements such as *Communione e Liberazione* and launched the *Studium Marcianum* in Venice, a school to promote Catholic identity in Italy and Europe. He is known throughout the many dioceses in the Third World and calls them "beacons for the Church of the future."

Cardinal Dionigi Tettamanzi

Archbishop of Milan.

Age: 71

One of the Church's foremost moral theologians and bioethicists, Cardinal Tettamanzi is shepherd of an archdiocese with some five million Catholics. Affable and known for his sense of humor and energy, he was a key figure in the preparation of Pope John Paul II's 1995 encyclical *Evangelium Vitae*. At the same time, he has enjoyed close relations with Opus Dei.

cially since quite a few names were of Cardinals from Asia, Africa, and Latin America.

The *Vaticanistas*

Still, conclaves, being the ancient institutions they are, remain capable of generating intense speculation, especially among the old established class of Vatican watchers and above all within the Italian press. By early in the week before the Cardinals gathered in the Sistine Chapel, various Italian newspapers (such as *La Stampa, Corriere della Serra,* and *La Repubblica*) were reporting rumors of how one Cardinal or another was rising to prominence while another might be dropping. The next day, the whole cycle would begin again.

What did prove lasting, however, was the presence of one name as a genuine contender, a name that had appeared on many *papabili* lists over the preceding months. Cardinal Joseph Ratzinger's name began circulating as a surprisingly strong candidate. The April 13th edition of *La Repubblica,* Rome's leading daily newspaper, published the view of noted *Vaticanista* Marco Politi that Cardinal Ratzinger commanded supposedly between 40 and 50 votes walking into the Conclave and was the clear front-runner through the support of powerful Cardinal Camillo Ruini of Rome, as well as Cardinal Angelo Scola of Venice, and three Cardinals from the Roman Curia, Cardinals Julián Herranz of Spain, and Alfonso López-Trujillo and Castrillón-Hoyos of Colombia. The weight of the story received apparent poundage by the release on April 2 of a book by Ratzinger, *Values in Times of Upheaval,* published by Munich's *Suddeutsche Zeitung,* noting one of the Cardinal's key themes, that of restoring Christian culture and faith in a Europe that has apparently abandoned both. Politi added that both Ruini and Scola were determined to block the possible candidacy of Cardinal Dionigi Tettamanzi of Milan and that another Italian candidate had emerged, namely Ennio Antonelli of Florence. Both *La Repubblica* and *Corriere della Serra* also reported that the two powerful German Cardinals, Karl Lehmann of Mainz and a Curial official, Walter Kasper, were vehemently opposed to Ratzinger.

This was followed by a second article in which Politi had declared that Vatican Secretary of State Cardinal Angelo Sodano was becoming a strong alternative to Ratzinger but that Kasper had gained some strength owing to his extensive work in the area of ecumenical dialogue, especially with the Russian Orthodox. Adding further to the mix was the publication of another book, this one by Cardinal Ruini, *Nuovi segni dei Tempi. La sorte della fede nell'età dei mutamenti* (New Signs of the Times: Faith in the Age of Change) by the publisher Mondadori, another volume on the crisis in culture and the threats posed by modernity.

Yet another intensely detailed analysis was provided by *Inside the Vatican*'s Dr. Robert Moynihan after his extensive discussions with the Italian journalist and noted Vatican watcher Sandro Magister. Magister's exposition on the state of affairs heading into the conclave was a masterpiece of logical speculation, weaving together a host of scenarios, names of *papabili,* and interpretations of the Cardinals' perspectives regarding the needs of the Church. As Moynihan reported on April 15, in his "Inside the Vatican Newsflash,"

> This, then, is the situation. Ratzinger is very strong right now. He is a bit old at 78. Some Italians and the more "progressive" faction oppose him, with Tettamanzi or Antonelli as an alternative. Ratzinger could hand off to his pupil, Scola. Scola could hand off to Bergoglio. Tettamanzi and Antonelli could hand off to Sodano, as an alternative to Ratzinger-Ruini-Scola, then, deadlocked, perhaps to Hummes, as they oscillate between Italy and Latin America. If Hummes vs. Bergoglio (for example) deadlocked, the Ratzinger group could again try Europe with Schönborn, while the more "progressive" Italian/Latin American group could try Maradiaga of Honduras. Some in Rome would still like to look toward Dias of India, but this might be a feint in order to rally support against Ratzinger and, having cut him off, putting Tettamanzi forward.

> So it went.

The Cardinals Reflect

For the Cardinals themselves, the experience of the conclave was the first for nearly all of them and they treated the undertaking as both a spiritual duty and a time of genuine prayer and reflection on the needs of the Church at the start of the third millennium. The members of the College who had assembled had met each other at various gatherings, but much of their time together in the General Congregations and in the quiet times before and after was spent getting to know each other better and listening to the opinions and perspectives of their fellow members. Cardinal Lubomyr Husar, Metropolitan Archbishop of Lviv and a prelate who had appeared on several list of *papabili*, spoke bluntly about the situation in an April 6 interview with Catholic News Service when he said that there were too many Cardinals in attendance to know each other very well.

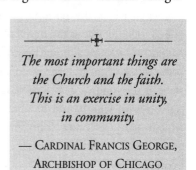

The most important things are the Church and the faith. This is an exercise in unity, in community.

— CARDINAL FRANCIS GEORGE, ARCHBISHOP OF CHICAGO

The need for opportunities to become better acquainted was not surprising given the sheer number of the Sacred College's members in 2005 compared to 1978 (183 to 125), although the number of Cardinal Electors was not that different (117 to 111). There was also the reality that some 60 of the Cardinals had been named in the last three years through the consistories of 2001 and 2003. A testament to the fact that the Cardinals did not know each other that well was manifested by the need for nametags for the first sessions of the closed consistory anticipating the public consistory of October 21, 2003, at which the last group of Cardinals was presented with their *zuchetti* and *birette*.

Thus, while the Cardinals were taking up the prayerful task of preparing for the vote, they also followed a two-track process of learning more about each other and studying the state of the Church globally from the experts who addressed them in their General Congregations. For example, regarding the gathering on April 13, Marco Politi reported that the 137 Cardinals in attendance had been briefed very thoroughly for three hours on the world situation politically and diplomatically (Politi added that Sodano did not mention the opposition of the Holy See to the United States' invasion of Iraq in 2003).

When not in their General Congregations, the Cardinals were also meeting together quietly — in the residences of the Cardinals in Rome, in the many national seminaries, and in restaurants. They talked together about the needs of the Church. Both law and custom forbid active campaigning by a Cardinal, but discussions sought to bring into harmony a triad of concerns: the will of the Holy Spirit, the state of the Church at the present moment in time, and finding the right person who would be able to meet those demands and prove truly worthy to follow John Paul II. Such small get-togethers had always been crucial in setting the direction for a subsequent conclave because it was here in the quiet of conversation that personalities could be discerned, reflections on ecclesiastical matters revealed, and genuine friendships established between prelates who might have only met a few times in previous consistories or irregular travel and symposia.

Finally, the Cardinals were able to do something together that was of the greatest importance. They shared together in the Masses of the *Novemdiales* and in the prayers throughout the day as they met in large assemblies and smaller gatherings. The spiritual bond that they forged was expressed well by Cardinal Francis George of Chicago when asked about the possibility of national or regional interests appearing in the conclave in the form of blocs, "I think any bloc would be resented. . . . The most important things are the Church and the faith. This is an exercise in unity, in community. To introduce a nation-state into that dynamic would be unfaithful to it."

While the Cardinals invoked a unanimous silence upon each other, there were nevertheless some glimpses as to what the Cardinals were actually thinking and who they might be looking at to succeed John Paul II. As they had set out from home and then spent several tiring days preparing to send off their friend and their pontiff, virtually all of the Cardinals had something to say about the deceased Pope and also — to varying degrees of openness — about the man who would follow.

The Cardinals kept their thoughts and comments deliberately vague, and no Cardinal suggested a name or even gave a description of a specific prelate who might be in mind. A common theme was to note the key role played by the Holy Spirit in any conclave and the need for trust in the work of the Holy Spirit in guiding the life of the Church. Precious few, such as the French Cardinal Philippe Barbarin of Lyon, said that they had arrived knowing already for whom they were voting.

Cardinal Husar tried immediately to demystify the process. In his interview with Catholic News Service on April 6, he commented that a papal election is serious business, but "let's not over-dramatize this. It is a serious responsibility because it is a serious job, but it is not as if the whole world depends on this. But the consequences are serious." As for the ideal candidate, he stressed that someone must fill the office of Pope, but each pontiff differs from those who had come before. For him, the key was for the new Pope to be prayerful and, he added, "He must be a man . . . I am very much against mystifying this. The person elected must say, 'I am who I am and God will do the rest.'" The key, he concluded, was not to create some profile and try to fill it with the candidate in the room who best fits it. But the next Pope should be a pastoral leader, a description that pointed to a bishop or archbishop of a major see where pastoral care is a priority. Cardinal Justin Rigali of Philadelphia shared Cardinal Husar's urging for a pastoral person, one who would be able to reach out to the entire world in solidarity and in charity. The pastoral experience was also a must for most Cardinals. That requirement did not rule out a Curial cardinal, however, for many of them had once been bishops of dioceses.

In an interview before reporters in Rome, Cardinal Francis George of Chicago enumerated several key characteristics, including the requirement of a Pope who is a man of faith, striving to be holy and faithful to Christ. He noted as well that a Pope must be able to speak Italian and be multilingual in keeping with his place as pastor of the Universal Church. While he did not have a specific person in mind, Cardinal George indicated that finding anyone capable of being Pope would be a challenge, but faith would permit him to be a true unifier. Faith is the same everywhere even as specific situations differ as do personalities. The unifying quality of faith, he added, "creates an enormous community, with compassion and empathy. Pope John Paul II had that. He was not Asian, but when he went to Asia he was an Asian. When he went to Latin America, he became Latin American. Not because he was an actor, but because he was a man of faith, and God is everywhere."

Cardinal Barbarin added, though, in an interview for French radio, that the key was finding someone who would be able to show the light of Christ and the vitality of the Gospel; far less important to the Cardinal was how old the Pope was or from what country he might come. "He must," the Cardinal said, "be able to communicate with the wealthy, the young in countries like the United States and France. Then he must be able to relate to the poor when he goes to places like Brazil or Morocco or Burkina Faso. He must be a person who can explain the Gospels to every kind of audience. He must truly love his flock and must understand their sufferings and their difficulties." He added, "John Paul II was that kind of Pope." This image was echoed by American Cardinal Edward Egan of New York and again by Cardinal George.

Another attribute cited frequently was the need for the next Pope to be himself and not try simply to be another John Paul II. Every new Pope brings his own talents, pastoral style, and gifts, and the new pontiff, the Cardinals agreed, needed to be true to those and not become a copy of the previous pontiff, as Cardinal Marc Ouellet of Quebec, Canada, put it, regardless of the immense skills and legacy of John Paul II. That perspective was repeated by Cardinal Godfried Danneels of Mechelen-Brussels, Belgium. Cardinal Egan, quoted in a Catholic News Service article added, "whoever is chosen . . . he would be very, very poorly advised to try to be Pope John Paul II, Paul VI, or Pius XII." In effect, a new Pope must be an authentic person.

Cardinal Darmaatmadja commented upon reaching Rome that John Paul II gave a remarkable lesson to his successor in his political courage and ability to make the Church a genuine force for morality in the world. The Pope had been a true moral leader and a respected, even loved, figure who reached every class. In Indonesia, for example, the Pope's passing was marked by messages of condolences from the heads of the government and Islamic leaders, but they were also sent by the association of motorbike drivers, among the poorest workers in the country. That model of authenticity that could reach across every barrier, every culture, and every religion must, the Cardinal urged, be carried forward by the next Pope.

Finally, the Cardinals seemed open and willing to consider a candidate from anywhere in the Church. Nevertheless, there seemed from the moment the *sede vacante* began to be an effort not to engage in conjecture regarding some requirement for the next Pope to be from a particular country or region. Dismissed too were thoughts — as Cardinal George had himself dismissed — of voting blocs by nation, pitting Third-World Cardinals against those of the First World, or some effort by Italian Cardinals to reclaim the papacy for their own.

Taken together, the Cardinals expressed their hope of finding a Cardinal from among their number who was a man of holiness, deep faith, and pastoral sensitivity. Additional characteristics were the need for languages, authenticity as a person, and the ability to connect with the entire world on a deeply personal level. Cardinal Fiorenzo Angelini, almost ninety and as such ineligible to take part in the conclave, also added a valuable reminder to the members of the press eager for any detail about prospective candidates. As he said to Catholic News Service, "I'm sure whatever predictions you journalists have collected will be swept away in one minute by the breath of the Holy Spirit."

Chapter 3

THE CONCLAVE'S ISSUES
⸺ ✠ ⸺

At this time, however, let us above all pray insistently to the Lord that after his great gift of Pope John Paul II, he will once again give us a Pastor according to his own heart, a Pastor who will guide us to knowledge of Christ, to His love, and to true joy.

— CARDINAL JOSEPH RATZINGER,
HOMILY, MASS FOR THE ELECTION OF THE ROMAN PONTIFF

The Tasks Ahead

Far more complicated than the generalized statements of the Cardinals regarding personal attributes were the estimates of the Cardinals of what were the key issues facing the Catholic Church at the start of the third millennium. There was no general sense of failure on the part of John Paul II (save for the views expressed in some quarters of the Church that saw his papacy as a hindrance to what they saw as authentic reform), nor was there an unrealistic view of the pontificate as itself being complete.

As with any Pope's reign, the pontificate of Pope John Paul II left some business unfinished. It had begun with his election as Pope in a world very different from the one he had left. The Soviet Union seemed firmly entrenched on the global landscape of politics. Marxist ideology and revolution were spreading across parts of Central and South America and Africa. Priests, nuns, and theologians were becoming attracted to extreme forms of liberation theology and applying Marxist interpretations to the spread of the Gospel. Within the Church, doubts and uncertainties in the years after the Second Vatican Council (1962-1965) raised questions about the long-term stability of Catholic institutions and the direction of the papacy itself.

John Paul had steered a straight course for the Barque of Peter from the first night of his election. Christianity, the Pope proclaimed, offers the only hope of true freedom, writing in the first encyclical of the pontificate, *Redemptor Hominis*, "Our spirit is set in one direction; the only direction for our intellect, will, and heart is toward Christ our Redeemer." Human dignity, he proclaimed, can be understood only in light of Christ, so that the human person must be defended against all threats to true freedom and dignity by the political and philosophical systems of the modern age. The task for the Church, as the Pope saw it, was to explain to the modern world both the importance of that freedom and its wide-ranging implications for the dignity and the rights of the human person.

By the end of the 1990s the Soviet Union had collapsed, the Church was growing steadily in Eastern Europe, and his own native Poland had tasted freedom for the first time since 1939. The Pope was able to travel to his jubilant homeland in August 1991. While he celebrated with his own people, he did not take justified credit for his role in the defeat of communism. Instead, he had stern words of warning to the new Poland: not to succumb to the fleeting and empty promises of the culture of death.

The Pope's visit to Poland in 1991 was a kind of turning point for the pontificate. Even as the pontiff had been dealing with the expiring ideology of communism, he was deeply

---

✠

In various parts of Europe a first proclamation of the Gospel is needed: *the number of the unbaptized is growing, both because of the significant presence of immigrants of other religions and because children born into families of Christian tradition have not received baptism, either as a result of the Communist domination or the spread of religious indifference.*

— POPE JOHN PAUL II,
APOSTOLIC EXHORTATION
ECCLESIA IN EUROPA

aware of the threats to freedom in the West from secular humanism, religious indifference, materialism, pornography, abortion, and other pressing issues of sexual morality. Offering a profound vision for a renewal of Catholic moral theology, John Paul wrote the encyclical *Veritatis Splendor* (1993), followed by the encyclical *Evangelium Vitae* (1995) in which he was unequivocal in reaffirming the Church's teaching on matters of reproduction while providing new insights into the nature of the family, the relationship between husband and wife, and the vital sacredness of all life.

At the same time, confronting the challenges of modern labor, capitalism, and economic justice, he published the encyclicals *Laborem Exercens* (1981), *Sollicitudo Rei Socialis* (1987), and *Centesimus Annus* (1991). He also challenged directly the underlying philosophies of our time in his 1998 encyclical *Fides et Ratio*, with the powerful words, "What human reason seeks 'without knowing it' (cf. Acts 17:23) can be found only through Christ."

In his call for fidelity to the teachings of the Second Vatican Council, John Paul focused much of his attention in governing the Church on the dual tasks of authentic reform and positive restatement of Church teaching. John Paul saw the Church not in a static defensive posture but in fidelity to the call of the Gospel to preach to all nations. As one of the most active members of the Second Vatican Council, the Pope knew that the council had mandated a dialogue with the modern world. In the long conversation of his reign, he spoke for the Church and apologized for the past errors of its members, and he pleaded for the reunion of the splintered Christian family.

He presided over a number of key documents on bioethics, liberation theology, the Church's inability to ordain women as priests, and the matter of dissent. In 1990, he issued the Constitution *Ex Corde Ecclesiae*, seeking to improve the orthodox commitment of Catholic universities. With his approval, the Congregation for the Doctrine of the Faith also released the document *Dominus Iesus*, in 2000, reiterating the words of *Lumen Gentium* concerning the central place of salvation in the Church.

The list of monumental achievements was thus an immensely long one, and the Church was left manifestly strengthened for his pontificate. Still, even a reign of such length does not take place in a historical vacuum. The papacy that began in the Cold War ended in the war against international terrorism. A pontificate that was inaugurated with bioethics still in its infancy ended with the ever growing nightmare of cloning, euthanasia, and embryonic research poised to kill millions in the name of scientific progress. And a reign that started with the Church still largely in its infancy in parts of the Third World finished with the Church playing a major role in shaping the very future of entire continents ravaged by AIDS, debt, globalization, and political instability. These did not point to failures on the part of the Pope. Indeed, he was a prophetic voice pleading for the world to listen to Jesus Christ as it plunged headlong into another century of war and chaos.

The history of the papacy is replete with such handing on of great tasks to new Popes. A century before Pope John Paul II, Bl. Pope Pius IX, upon his death, also left much still to be done: building on the Catholic missions around the world; improving relations with the states of Europe; finding the way forward to preserve the temporal power of the papacy against a hostile Italian government; making further ground in the effort to resist the proliferation of the toxic philosophies of the age; and above all, proclaiming the Gospel in new ways in the face of the Industrial Revolution. One of history's greatest pontiffs, who enjoyed a reign of 32 years, left it to Leo XIII to continue his tasks. In his own turn, Leo left to Pope St. Pius X his own set of challenges and opportunities.

Media Expectations

In the final years of the pontificate of Pope John Paul II, the Western media were filled with columns and articles on what the Cardinals would consider the most pressing issues facing the Church as they pondered the attributes and requisite skills for the new Pope. The coverage swung across the spectrum of theological positions, from the so-called far right to the far left. The preponderance of emphasis was one of hopefulness that the next Pope would bring the changes to the Church that the writers and analysts envisioned from their own positions. The result was often a focus on what can be termed ecclesiastical provincialism, the notion that the favorite doctrinal issues that were important to the writers were necessarily vital to the future of the entire Church simply because they saw them as crucial in one region or even one country. The predictable laundry list of desired changes included increased power-sharing in the Church, the ordination of women, the end to clerical celibacy, and changes on traditional Church teachings on abortion, contraception, and homosexuality.

These same issues received the weight of the coverage from many analysts on the major television networks, cable news outlets, and print media. On one cable news program, for example, a leader of a dissenting organization of self-proclaimed Catholics in the United States declared her belief that the Cardinals' chief task was to do away with the entire legacy of Pope John Paul II as a failure and to introduce the changes that her own small group was advocating for the Church.

What was most striking about the coverage in the majority of media outlets was the apparent disconnect between the speculation of experts and what the Cardinals and world's bishops were discussing at their ordinary and extraordinary gatherings in the final years of Pope John Paul II's reign. The picture of what the Cardinals saw as the most dire and important issues for the conclave was thus rather different from the one broadcast across the globe in the months and days before the Cardinals entered the Sistine Chapel.

Further forecast for many of the key issues was provided in May 2001 when 155 Cardinals, the largest such consistory in Church history, gathered in Rome with the purpose not of electing the next Pope but of discussing the future of the Church in the third millennium. While the agenda was officially declared to be one of anticipating the needs and tasks of the Church for the new century and beyond, much of the pre-consistory anticipation was that it would provide the Cardinals with an opportunity to get to know each other and to make initial assessments for an impending conclave.

Most journalists and observers made the assumption that the Cardinals would be arriving with a focus on such issues as collegiality, subsidiarity, and the laundry list of issues dear to some in the West. At the consistory in May 2001, the Cardinals touched upon collegiality, but it was placed as one issue of several being considered. These included stressing holiness in the life of the Christian, the place of the papal ministry, promoting missionary outreach, strengthening marriage and family life, the challenges of globalization and economic justice, and working toward ecumenism and interreligious dialogue.

That same year, the 10th ordinary general assembly of the Synod of Bishops was held from September 30 to October 27, 2001 under the title of "The Bishop: Servant of the Gospel of Jesus Christ for the Hope of the World." The synod was considered especially urgent since it convened only weeks after the terror attacks on 9/11. The 250 bishops who attended the synod read in the media during the weeks preceding the first sessions less about the terrorist attacks and more about the impending struggles between Rome and the world's bishops over collegiality and moral theology.

The interventions of the many bishops revealed the wide-ranging concerns that they brought with them from their particular churches, especially as they related to the role and charism of the bishop. Where the Synod in 1999 anticipated the global condition toward the end of John Paul II's pontificate, the Synod in 2001 began speaking to the characteristics needed by the bishop who would inevitably assume the burdens of the papacy. Cardinal Castrillón Hoyos declared:

> The bishop dominated by fear will not be the man of the Gospel, nor the man of hope. Scared in front of public opinion, he does not preserve the faith with the opportunity for correction ... The bishop as teacher educates, as a leader corrects, as a liturgical person celebrates the divine cult; as a leader he is

firm when facing abuses, as a teacher he preaches morals, as a leader he unveils and corrects failures and keeps traditions. The bishop, leader of the diocesan community, does not stop committing himself so that Christ's thinking may find a place in public life.

In the post-synodal apostolic exhortation of Pope John Paul II, *Pastores Gregis*, which reflected upon the work of the 2001 Synod, the role of the bishop was described vividly:

> The Bishop is called in a particular way to be a prophet, witness, and servant of hope. He has the duty of instilling confidence and proclaiming before all people the basis of Christian hope (cf. 1 Pet 3:15). The Bishop is the prophet, witness and servant of this hope, especially where a culture of "the here and now" leaves no room for openness to transcendence. Where hope is absent, faith itself is called into question. Love too is weakened by the loss of this virtue. Especially in times of growing unbelief and indifference, hope is a stalwart support for faith and an effective incentive for love. It draws its strength from the certainty of God's desire for the salvation of all people (cf. 1 Tim 2:4) and from the constant presence of the Lord Jesus, the *Emmanuel* who remains with us always, until the end of the world (cf. Mt 28:20).

The Key Themes

For those who had listened to the words of the Bishops and Cardinals rather than the pundits who tried to explain them through the lens of the progressive or conservative perspective — the limited comments of the Cardinals who gathered in Rome for the conclave continued to speak of the issues that had been explored from 1999 to 2005. The statements revealed the collective mind of the Church's leadership on the needs of the Church, and as the Cardinals spoke, the key themes and issues came into focus.

Cardinal George Pell established some useful parameters when he said to reporters before the ban on speaking to the press, "I think Pope John Paul is a bit of a miracle, and I don't think anybody's expecting two miracles in a row." Having noted that, he suggested a group of issues that he and his fellow members of the Sacred College were likely to be discussing in the coming General Congregations: decline of faith, particularly in Europe with its direct challenge to the central place of Christ and basic belief in God; the proliferation of the culture of death in such areas as abortion, euthanasia, and contraception with its severe impact on the population of the West; the challenge of relations with Islam and the need for constructive dialogue; and a missionary zeal to reach into Asia, especially in the wake of economic development. He then went on to consider as secondary in importance such issues as aspects of Church governance and the relationship between the particular churches and the Universal Church.

A slightly different emphasis was placed on issues by Franciscan Cardinal Claudio Hummes of São Paulo, Brazil. As he said in late 2004, "Jesus was born poor among the poor to call our attention to the social injustice that makes a portion of humanity increasingly poor, suffering, humiliated, and excluded from sufficient access to the goods of the earth." In a notable address he delivered in March 2005 at the conference "The Call to Justice: The Legacy of *Gaudium et Spes* 40 Years Later" at the Vatican on the Second Vatican Council document, *Gaudium et Spes*, on the Church in the modern world, he situated the Church's efforts on proclaiming the Gospel in those regions facing staggering poverty, disease, and political oppression. Such, Hummes suggests, is an emphasis on social engagement in which the Church does not seek to impose solutions but to engage in dialogue. He stated:

> The Church must constantly promote dialogue. Perhaps it is among the most important methods today for positive and constructive relations with society ... A dialogue with the contemporary person, with the human race, science, the advances in biotechnology, with philosophy and the cultures, with poli-

tics and economics, with everything that has to do with social justice, with human rights, and with solidarity with the poor. A dialogue with the religions. A constant dialogue, systematic, with professionalism, constructive. A dialogue that knows how to listen, to debate, to discern, and to assimilate whatever is good and true, just, and consistent with human dignity, proposed by the interlocutor. A dialogue that at the same time knows how to proclaim the truth of which the church is the depository, and to which it must remain permanently faithful. However, it must always remain a dialogue, and never an imposition of the church's own convictions and methods. Propose, not impose. To serve, and not to dominate . . .

The faith must express itself in charity and in solidarity, which is the civil form of charity. Today more than ever, the church faces this challenge. In fact, effective solidarity with the poor, both individual persons and entire nations, is indispensable for the construction of peace. Solidarity corrects injustices, reestablishes the fundamental rights of persons and of nations, overcomes poverty, and even resists the revolt that injustice provokes, eliminating the violence that is born with revolt and constructing peace.

Cardinal George focused on both of the key issues mentioned by Cardinals Pell and Hummes through what he called aggressive secularism and the "scandal of the continuing gap between rich and poor." He then suggested two other key issues: relations with Islam and the challenge of moral conditions in modern society, including biotechnology and changing sexual mores. When asked by a reporter if he thought the Cardinals of the United States would support a Pope who might end the Church's opposition to birth control in order to help end such problems as poverty, Cardinal George replied, "So your solution is to exterminate the poor in order to take care of poverty?"

Cardinals Pell and Hummes were not in any disagreement on the call of the Gospel to be preached everywhere. Where they differed was in the placement of specific emphasis. Cardinal George united the two perspectives and added several key factors related to them. Cardinal George thus pointed to the two great concerns of the Cardinals as their discussions progressed in the days before the conclave: the crisis of culture and faith in the First World and the colossal challenges of poverty and population growth in the Third World.

The two concerns were not isolated from each other and both were crucial problems to be faced by the next Pope; neither can be ignored, and progress in both areas will be essential for the long-term advancement of the faith in the coming century. The degree to which these two seemingly disparate problems are interwoven was made clear by Pope John Paul II in his key 2001 document *Novo Millennio Ineunte* ("At the Start of the Third Millennium"):

> Our world is entering the new millennium burdened by the contradictions of an economic, cultural, and technological progress which offers immense possibilities to a fortunate few, while leaving millions of others not only on the margins of progress but in living conditions far below the minimum demanded by human dignity. How can it be that even today there are still people dying of hunger? Condemned to illiteracy? Lacking the most basic medical care? Without a roof over their heads?
>
> The scenario of poverty can extend indefinitely, if in addition to its traditional forms we think of its newer patterns. These latter often affect financially affluent sectors and groups which are nevertheless threatened by despair at the lack of meaning in their lives, by drug addiction, by fear of abandonment in old age or sickness, by marginalization or social discrimination. In this context, Christians must learn to make their act of faith in Christ by discerning his voice in the cry for help that rises from this world of poverty. This means carrying on the tradition of charity which has expressed itself in so many different ways in the past two millennia, but which today calls for even greater resourcefulness. Now is the time for a new "creativity" in charity, not only by ensuring that help is effec-

tive but also by "getting close" to those who suffer, so that the hand that helps is seen not as a humiliating handout but as a sharing between brothers and sisters.

The Church in the West

John Paul II was prophetic in his concerns for the future of the Church, and he rightly noted in his last days that a dark shadow seemed to be enshrouding the world. Darkness is present especially in the collapse of faith in Europe and elsewhere in the First World, with the attendant risks posed in the progress of the culture of death — abortion, euthanasia, pornography, and cloning.

In Western Europe alone, affluence, secularization, and the steady erosion of a sense of personal faith have resulted in the collapse of church attendance among all faiths and in the steady decline in births through abortion, contraception, and the choice by parents to postpone children in order to enjoy the toys and distractions that modern culture provides in lieu of a true family. The Catholic population alone has declined by nearly 3.4 million between 1997 and 2002, and across Europe the demographics present a grim picture for the future. Without a replacement population, the tax burden has fallen increasingly upon a dwindling worker base. To answer the need for workers, European countries employed an open door policy for immigration from Eastern Europe, North Africa, and the Middle East. While providing opportunities for families from those regions, the result is a demographic tidal wave and a sharp change in the religious make-up of countries in the West. In France, which is still 78% Catholic, the second largest religion is now Islam. Similarly, Islam is the fastest growing religion in all of Europe, eclipsing by a considerable margin the Protestant denominations in Northern Europe where the population declines have been especially felt.

Northern Europe, too, most so in the Netherlands, has become ground zero for the culture of death. Euthanasia, abortion, pornography of every description, child pornography rings, open prostitution, and sterilizations are commonplace. Dutch physicians euthanize infants born with cleft palates and various birth defects. The churches are largely empty during services, and the sense of faith and Christian culture are barely visible beneath the weight of the new European self-image. Nowhere was it more apparent than in the deliberations of the European Union during its drafting of the constitution when any recognition of the Christian roots of Europe was defeated.

Pope John Paul II expressed the thoughts of the Synod of Bishops concerning the growing dangers of secularization and the death of faith when he wrote in his apostolic exhortation *Ecclesia in Europa* (2003):

> Many of the baptized live as if Christ did not exist: the gestures and signs of faith are repeated, especially in devotional practices, but they fail to correspond to a real acceptance of the content of the faith and fidelity to the person of Jesus. The great certainties of the faith are being undermined in many people by a vague religiosity lacking real commitment; various forms of agnosticism and practical atheism are spreading and serve to widen the division between faith and life; some people have been affected by the spirit of an immanentist humanism, which has weakened the faith and often, tragically, led to its complete abandonment; one encounters a sort of secularist interpretation of Christian faith which is corrosive and accompanied by a deep crisis of conscience and of Christian moral practice.

But what were the Cardinals thinking? In October 1999, the Second European Synod of Bishops was held at the Vatican on the theme "Jesus Christ, Alive in His Church, Source of Hope for Europe." The bishops who assembled to discuss the crises and challenges facing Europe began under a cloud as the speeches tended to project an image of gloom and decline for Christian culture in virtually every corner of the continent. Cardinal López Trujillo, President of the Pontifical Council for the Family, for example, lamented the "systematic demolition" of family life, while others enumerated the domination of European culture by materialism and secularism as well as the steep declines in Mass attendance, vocations, and active participation in the parish and diocese.

The darkness, however, was lifted starkly by the series of later interventions that called upon the Church to be less concerned with structures of governance and more concerned with proclaiming the Gospel. Cardinal Dionigi Tettamanzi declared, "The priority for our Church today is not baptizing new converts but converting those already baptized."

In keeping with the sudden spirit of the synod, the call for a wider form of collegial gathering — taken by observers to be a suggestion for an ecumenical council — that was expressed by Carlo Cardinal Martini, then Archbishop of Milan, received a cool reception, and his eventual successor at Milan, Cardinal Tettamanzi, made the observation that the idea "did not find an echo within the synod assembly." Even more direct was Archbishop Josef Zycinski of Kraków, who declared at a press conference, "Existing structures are more than adequate for preaching the Good News ... The difficulties confronting the Church today will not be resolved through magic or demagogy, but rather through new forms of preaching ..."

In its Message to the European People approved on October 22, 1999, the Synod participants ended their gathering on a hopeful note: "Church of Europe, fear not! The God of hope will not abandon you! Believe in His salvific love. Trust in His mercy which forgives, revives and renews. Rely on your Lord and you will never be lost for eternity."

Cardinal Ruini addressed the issue of faith in Europe in an extensive interview with Sandro Magister that was published originally in *L'Espresso* in 2002. Regarding the state of Europe, Cardinal Ruini maintained,

> de-Christianization without a doubt is advancing. It's a long-term process that is very significant. And it imposes on the Church a need to change ... Rather than mission, Pope John Paul II has spoken of new evangelization. Mission brings to mind a "*tabula rasa*," in which the Gospel has to be planted

from scratch. But new evangelization takes place in terrain already nourished by Christianity, in which the great Christian heritage is threatened and disputed but persists. The Gospel that is proclaimed is the same here and in pagan lands, but the context is different. Man is different.

The task for the next Pope as spelled out by those Cardinals in the forefront of the struggle with modernity and finding a way for the Gospel to flourish in the West is an enormous one. Not only does the new pontiff face the task of sparking a renewal in culture and the family, he must confront the steady decline in vocations to the priesthood and religious life, the divergence of Catholics from Church teaching, the ongoing discussion of collegiality, and the open promotion of dissent on core teachings permitted in Catholic universities. There are also the lingering effects of the sex-abuse scandal, the reform of Catholic seminaries, and the pervasive anti-Catholic atmosphere in the media.

The consequences of failure would be far-reaching. Indeed, the future of an authentically Christian West is at stake, one that values human life from conception to natural death; so too is the continued development of the Church in Asia, Africa, and Latin America. The dioceses and archdioceses of the West, most so the United States and Germany, are crucial to the funding of efforts at evangelization in Africa and South and Central America, as well as the construction of seminaries, convents, schools, rectories, and orphanages for the countless children left without parents because of the AIDS crisis.

The collapse of faith and culture in Europe is felt even in the developing regions and is a hindrance to evangelization. In the face of Islam, Catholic teachers and missionaries, as well as native clergy and laity, are asked to explain why the Catholic faith is not practiced anymore in the lands that brought it to their country. As Cardinal Peter Turkson of Cape Coast, Ghana, declared in an interview with Catholic News Service, "if the image of the church in Europe is of a dying church, it gives us an orphaned feeling. It is important that the Church in Europe come back alive."

On this basis, the suggestion was made by some analysts and papal experts that a European Cardinal might be chosen by sheer necessity for the Church to begin the task of bringing a new springtime to Europe. They point to the progress already started under John Paul II and cite the emergence of ecclesial movements such as Opus Dei, Communion and Liberation, and Focolare. While some complain that they are exclusivist in their tendencies, they are much supported by many Cardinals, such as Dionigi Tettamanzi with his ties to Opus Dei and Angelo Scola of Venice with his long association with Fr. Luigi Giussani and Communion and Liberation. Cardinal Ruini addressed the issue of such movements by giving assurance that "the most lively ones are maturing, and with time they will integrate more and more into the fabric of the church. In fact, they already are giving many positive fruits with their drive for Christian identity and mission." In addition, there are other positive signs in the stunning attendance of European youth at World Youth Days, the slight increases in vocations to the priesthood and religious life, and, anecdotally, the attendance in truly large numbers of young people at the papal funeral.

The Developing World

Against this argument was the prophetic statement of the late Cardinal Laurean Rugambwa, the first African Cardinal named in the 20th century and Archbishop of Dar-es-Salaam, Tanzania, that the day would come when the Church in Africa would re-evangelize the West. His words pointed powerfully to the growth of the Catholic faith in the developing world and the remarkable success in the pontificate of John Paul II to reach out to the poorest nations and offer hope and the love of Christ.

The developing world is in dire need of the Gospel's hope for millions who live in poverty and are viewed as mere human resources to powerful capitalist countries; where epidemics such as AIDS, Ebola, and Marburg prey on the helpless; where tens of thousands of children starve to death and die from common illnesses, and where civil wars and corrupt regimes oppress the helpless.

The numbers themselves tell a striking tale. Where populations, including Catholic ones, are shrinking in Western Europe, the population is growing swiftly in the developing world and the Catholic population is keeping pace. Of the Catholic Church's one billion members, over 700 million are in the developing world. Of those, over 450 million are found in Latin America, so that rapidly half of the Catholics in the world will live in Central and South America. In Asia, there are over 110 million Catholics, including 65 million in the Philippines alone. The Church in Africa in 1955 claimed sixteen million members; today there are over 137 million. Of the countries with the largest Catholic populations, the five largest are Brazil, Mexico, the United States, the Philippines, and Italy. (See box below.) In effect, the future of the Church is in the southern hemisphere.

Added to this demographic reality is the marked increase in the United States of Latino populations. It is projected that in 2020, the Hispanic population will be approximately 52.7 million; by 2040, the population will be about 80.2 million; by 2050 the population will be 96.5 million, comprising approximately 24.5 percent of the entire U.S. population. The Church in the United States thus shares in the shift apparent elsewhere in the world.

The World's Largest Catholic Countries

Brazil	149,329,000	(85%)
Mexico	92,220,269	(92%)
United States	67,259,768	(23%)
Philippines	65,063,000	(83%)
Italy	55,763,000	(97%)
France	46,110,000	(78%)
Colombia	38,701,000	(89%)
Spain	38,437,000	(94%)
Poland	36,977,000	(96%)
Argentina	34,224,000	(90%)
Germany	27,401,000	(33.2%)

The raw statistics of the Catholic growth in the Third World do little to provide a picture of the vitality of the faith, just as it can do faint justice to the overwhelming challenges faced by the Church in those regions. The Catholic Church in Latin America entered the new century with a heightened sense of purpose and organization. Gone for the most part was the long association of the institutional Church with the colonial governments of the Old World or the dictatorial regimes that so deeply troubled the continent and held back the energy, talents, and hope of the people. Over the last fifty years, the leaders of the Church have served as powerful and influential spokesmen for the Gospel. They have confronted military juntas, as did Claudio Hummes in Brazil, in his support of steel workers; they have offered a spiritual model for their country, as has Cardinal Jorge Mario Bergoglio in Argentina; and they have brokered negotiations between terrorists and governments, as seen with Cardinal Juan Luis Cipriani Thorne in Peru.

Still, Latin America suffers from severe poverty, a continuing disparity between the rich and poor, so that children starve to death a few feet away from restaurants frequented by the wealthy and influential. The Church continues to grapple as well with native religions, such as Umbanda, that pose risks of syncretist tendencies among Catholics, and serious inroads from the Pentecostal Movement. Cardinal Hummes has been especially effective in São Paulo resisting defections from the Church to these sects, and one point often raised in favor of a Pope from Latin American is precisely the boost he would provide to those engaged in preventing departures and welcoming back those Catholic who return after a dalliance with such groups.

In Asia, where the Catholic population is less than 3%, the Church has faced severe persecutions in predominately Islamic countries, such as Indonesia and Pakistan. In India, Catholics are attacked, especially in the Malabar province by intolerant members of the Hindu majority. In this country of over one billion people, Catholics comprise a tiny but faithful and determined minority of 17 million.

Notable Cardinals in India are Ivan Dias, Archbishop of Bombay; Varkey Vithayathil, C.SS.R., the Major Archbishop of Ernakulam-Angamaly for Syro-Malabars; and Telesphore Placidus Toppo, Archbishop of Ranchi. Toppo was the first tribesman convert to become a Cardinal in India, and Dias was considered by some to be a genuine *papabile.*

Slower headway has been made in Japan where the Church remains less than one percent of the population and especially in China, where Christianity was attacked directly by the Communist regime under Mao Tse-tung and his successors through laws that outlawed missionary work and pastoral activity. The Communist government of China continues to deny the free exercise of religion and is responsible for the detention of hundreds of priests, religious, and lay people in jail and their employment in slave labor; the proscription of Catholic movements for "counterrevolutionary activities" and "crimes against the new China." Relations with China may well prove one of the great challenges and perhaps opportunities for the next Pope.

Finally, in Africa, the Church has flourished over the last half century, boasting over 22,000 seminarians and 50,000 women religious. Such are the numbers of vocations among the native clergy that seminaries cannot be built fast enough, classes are staggered for enrollment, and many seminarians are sent to study elsewhere. Even more significantly, African clergy and religious, like their Asian and Latin American counterparts, are being sent to the United States and Europe to serve in priestless parishes, empty convents, and other places for ministry.

In Africa, as in Asia, the Church also deals squarely with the dire crises of the age. The AIDS epidemic has killed millions, and Church resources are stretched to their breaking point by the charitable works undertaken by Catholic personnel to care for the victims and their orphans. Likewise, Catholic charitable efforts feed untold thousands, educate the young, and labor to bring hope in regions where none has been found for many years. The growing pains of a young Church have been felt in such countries as Uganda and Rwanda where

Catholics took part in the bloody genocidal civil war in the late 1990s. The political unrest of the continent was driven home by the murder on December 29, 2003, of Archbishop Michael Courtney, the papal nuncio to Burundi, by gunmen while traveling on the road to the nation's capital, Bujumbura.

Dangers are posed also, as in Asia and the Middle East, by the rise of militant elements in Islam. In Algeria, Nigeria, and elsewhere, missionaries are murdered, Christians are sold in the flourishing slave trade in Central Africa, and Catholics live under severe disabilities imposed by hard-line Islamic governments. In Algeria alone, armed Islamic militants and guerrillas have caused terror and unrest since 1992. Among the more than 80,000 people killed were seven Trappist monks and the Catholic Bishop of Oran, all in 1996. In Nigeria, the bishops have spoken out against the imposition of Islamic law in individual states within the country.

The staggering poverty, the political upheaval, the corruption of some African governments, and the dangers posed by Islam have not halted the success of evangelization. The Church in Africa is led by courageous bishops, priests, nuns and religious, and especially by lay men and women willing to give their lives for the faith.

Cardinal Hummes' line of reasoning — one echoed by many of the Cardinals — suggests that the world's great problems stem in large measure from the gulf between the rich and the poor, between the strong and the weak. This is true even in the realm of international terror. "Does not today's terrorism," he asked, "have as one of its ingredients a revolt against an imposed poverty, experienced as practically irreversible in the short and medium term?" As Pope John Paul II wrote in the Encyclical Letter *Centesimus Annus*: "The poor ask for the right to share in enjoying material goods and to make good use of their capacity to work, thus creating a world that is more just and prosperous for all. The advancement of the poor constitutes a great opportunity for the moral, cultural, and even economic growth of all humanity" (n. 28).

Two particular issues plague the relationship of the First and the Third Worlds, and both have been mentioned extensively in the words of Cardinals and in official statements of the Holy See over the last twenty years. The first is debt and the second is globalization. Pope John Paul II counted international debt in *Novo Millennio Ineunte*, writing:

> The question of multilateral debt contracted by poorer countries with international financial organizations has shown itself to be a rather more problematic issue. It is to be hoped that the member States of these organizations, especially those that have greater decisional powers, will succeed in reaching the necessary consensus in order to arrive at a rapid solution to this question on which the progress of many countries depends, with grave consequences for the economy and the living conditions of so many people (no.14).

In practical terms, the total external debt of developing countries increased from $1.5 trillion in 1990 to $2.4 trillion in 2001, but the effect of this debt was far more deleterious to the well-being of underdeveloped countries in that it causes a severe outflow of financial resources and the effective plundering of their vital natural resources that should be going to infrastructure and development, including basic health care, education, and economic improvement.

Archbishop Celestino Migliore, papal representative to the United Nations, addressed a committee of the U.N. General Assembly in 2003 on the topic "Crisis of External Debt and Development." He declared that international debt posed two special challenges. First, he noted, is the need to find overall solutions to the debt problem, and the second is establishing a lasting financial system that might be of use to every country. He emphasized the deeper meaning of the debt crisis: "Since human beings are endowed with the inherent capacity for moral choice, no human activity takes place outside the sphere of moral judgment. Therefore, those activities that have enduring consequences on the life of an entire population, particularly on its poorer segments, deserve particular attention and moral scrutiny."

Archbishop Migliore also urged the United Nations to heed the words of the Holy See regarding the development of the Third World. He cited three points:

- The right of development is inherent in every person, group, or nation, and the world's 370 million indigenous peoples have the same claim to development as all the rest.
- Development, to be truly human, should be integral, comprising all its multidimensional aspects: economic and social, political and cultural, moral and spiritual; it has to be both individual and collective, personal and shared.
- The indigenous peoples themselves must be architects of their own development.

Cardinal Rodríguez Maradiaga of Honduras, an outspoken advocate in solving the crisis of debt, has talked extensively on the problem of globalization as well. In addressing the internationalization of economies and the dangers it poses to underdeveloped countries falling prey to the wealthy and stronger economic powerhouses of the West, Rodríguez Maradiaga said in 2004 during an appearance at the University of St. Thomas in Houston, Texas, "If we accept the globalization of wealth, technology, and power, without the globalization of human rights and human dignity, then we have failed in our duties as educated Catholics." In an interview given to the magazine *30 Days* in September 2003, Cardinal Errázuriz Ossa of Santiago de Chile stated:

> The globalization of the economy, as it was done, has determined the fact that the poorest countries and peoples are sidelined by development. Globalization is a fact of life, inevitable, but it's not inevitable that it should lower the standard of living of the people already with very little. It depends on the model of globalization that is applied. We can and must hope that there is real globalization of solidarity, the criteria for

which are not only economico-financial but also create space for respect of the dignity of the economically underdeveloped.

For many Cardinals, then, the central issue facing the conclave was that of social justice and the severe disparity between wealthy and poor nations. Poverty, injustice, debt, and globalization are the keys to bringing peace and stability to a world growing closer through technology and international economics.

Finally, tied closely to the progress of the Church in both the First and Third Worlds is the issue of dealing with the religions of the world, especially Islam. Cardinal Francis Arinze, who had been head of the Pontifical Council for Interreligious Dialogue from 1985 to 2002, provided the essentials of dialogue when he wrote in *Meeting Other Believers* (Our Sunday Visitor, 1998):

> Interreligious Dialogue is a meeting of people of differing religions, in an atmosphere of freedom and openness, in order to listen to the other, to try to understand that person's religion, and hopefully to seek possibilities of collaboration. It is hoped that the other partner will reciprocate, because dialogue should be marked by a two-way and not a one-way movement. Reciprocity is in the nature of dialogue. There is give and take. Dialogue implies both receptivity and active communication.

As the Church has grown throughout the world, development has been attended by encounters with the other major faiths — Buddhism, Hinduism, and Islam. In addition, one of the great priorities of the last 40 years for the Church has been outreach to Judaism, since Bl. Pope John XXIII's endearing call for dialogue and the immense progress made under Pope John Paul II, including formal diplomatic relations with Israel in 1994. Relations in parts of the world with Hinduism and Buddhism have been troubled by strife, misunderstanding, and hostility — such as the brutal treatment of Christians by extremist Hindus in some states of India.

The most pressing concern, of course, is the relationship between the Church and Islam. The Muslim faith is, as has been seen, a growing presence in the West and a major force in many developing countries of Africa and Asia. In Western Europe and North America, the minaret of the mosque is appearing in greater numbers across cities such as Paris and London and even in such unexpected places as Rome and Indianapolis, Indiana. In Africa and Indonesia, the cultivation of dialogue and understanding are essential for the very survival of small minority communities of Catholics and other Christians.

Dialogue is, consequently, both necessary and desirable. Such a dialogue with Islam is not, as some have suggested in the wake of September 11, a "clash of civilizations." As Cardinal Ruini observed in his interview with *L'Espresso* in 2002, when asked about the possibility of a clash,

> That is a risk we must avoid at all costs, precisely by rediscovering and appreciating the Christian identity of Europe. This is in part because that identity is less alien to Islam than pure naturalism. But what matters more is that this Christian identity is intrinsically oriented toward love for those who are different, while remaining what it is itself. Christianity is capable of providing the cultural impulses for a future society that is free, peaceful, and pluralistic. This is an enormous new challenge, never seen in the past, but now unavoidable. And Christianity has within itself the strength to face it positively.

As the funeral of John Paul II showed, the fruits of dialogue with Islam included opening relations with Iran and other Islamic countries, an event once considered unthinkable. At the papal funeral were representatives of Iran and Syria, and during the pontificate of John Paul II diplomatic relations were established with such Muslim nations as Tajikistan (1996), Libya (1997), Yemen (1998), Bahrain (2000), Djibouti (2000), and Qatar (2002).

The challenge for the next Pope will be to find the right balance between promoting active dialogue and further progress in relations while defending the rights of Catholics in Islamic countries and advocating religious freedom. The effort will be complicated by the presence of large Muslim populations in predominately Catholic countries, such as France, where tensions can create outbreaks of intolerance and extremism on both sides. The Church opposed the headscarf ban imposed by the French government in 2003 on the basis that it violated religious freedom and might lead to additional bans on other forms of religious expression.

Equally, the next Pope will be aware of the obligation to preach the Gospel. As Cardinal Marco Cé, patriarch emeritus of Venice, suggested in an address to a congress organized by the Italian Federation of Catholic Weeklies (FISC) in 2004, relations between Christians and Muslims in Italy should be marked by not "rancorous argument, but a fraternal — and at the same time responsible and wise — welcome." The Cardinal added:

> We cannot hide the historical and cultural differences. However, in the past these have not impeded a symbiosis of civilizations, as in the European Middle Ages . . . in our country, in our cities, where the flow of migrations bring ever more numerous Muslim guests, many say disconsolately that the future will only bring conflict. We do not shut our eyes to difficulties, but we hold on to God's announcement to Abraham: prosperity and greatness for the descendants of Ishmael and Isaac . . . Integration cannot mean forgetfulness of one's religious identity, or fear of the free proclamation of the Gospel.

John Paul wrote of the place of outreach and dialogue in *Novo Millennio Ineunte*:

> Dialogue, however, cannot be based on religious indifferentism, and we Christians are in duty bound, while engaging in dialogue, to bear clear witness to the hope that is within us (cf. *1 Pt* 3:15). We should not fear that it will be considered an offence to the identity of others what is rather *the joyful proclamation of a gift* meant for all, and to be offered to all with the greatest respect for the freedom of each one: the gift of the revelation of the God who is Love, the God who "so loved the

world that he gave his only Son" (*Jn* 3:16). As the recent Declaration *Dominus Iesus* stressed, this cannot be the subject of a dialogue understood as negotiation, as if we considered it a matter of mere opinion: rather, it is a grace which fills us with joy, a message which we have a duty to proclaim.

The Church therefore cannot forgo her missionary activity among the peoples of the world. It is the primary task of the *missio ad gentes* to announce that it is in Christ, "the Way, and the Truth, and the Life" (Jn 14:6), that people find salvation. Interreligious dialogue "cannot simply replace proclamation, but remains oriented towards proclamation". This missionary duty, moreover, does not prevent us from approaching dialogue *with an attitude of profound willingness to listen.* We know in fact that, in the presence of the mystery of grace, infinitely full of possibilities and implications for human life and history, the Church herself will never cease putting questions, trusting in the help of the Paraclete, the Spirit of Truth (cf. Jn 14:17), whose task it is to guide her "into all the truth" (Jn 16:13) (no. 56).

The Cardinals thus had much on their minds as they processed through the Apostolic Palace toward the Sistine Chapel chanting the magnificent and ancient hymn *"Veni, Creator Spiritus."* Their work in the General Congregations, their dialogue with one another, and their gatherings in prayer and the celebration of the Eucharist had led them ultimately to this moment and their appointed task.

As the Cardinals walked into the Sistine Chapel they were greeted unavoidably by the majesty of Michelangelo's "Last Judgment," whose central figure is Christ. As the call was made by the Papal Master of Ceremonies, Archbishop Piero Marini, *"Extra Omnes!* ("Others Out!"), however, there was still one last factor very present in the atmosphere of the Chapel. Twenty-seven years had passed since the last time the College of Cardinals had gathered to perform this sacred function. Pope John Paul II had emerged from that conclave. Barely ten days had passed since his funeral, but the

cries of the faithful still echoed faintly along the Via della Conciliazione and throughout the ornate halls of Vatican City, *"Magnus!
Magnus!"* For all of the discussions about where the next Pope would
lead the Church, there was on inescapable truth before them. The
words of John Paul II were more apt in the Sistine Chapel on the
morning of April 18, 2005 than at any time during his own unprecedented papacy:

> It is not therefore a matter of inventing a "new program."
> The program already exists: it is the plan found in the Gospel
> and in the living Tradition, it is the same as ever. Ultimately, it
> has its center in Christ himself, who is to be known, loved and
> imitated, so that in him we may live the life of the Trinity, and
> with him transform history until its fulfilment in the heavenly
> Jerusalem. This is a program which does not change with shifts
> of times and cultures, even though it takes account of time and
> culture for the sake of true dialogue and effective communica-
> tion. This program for all times is our program for the third
> millennium (*Novo Millennio Ineunte*, 29).

Just as had occurred in 1978, the Cardinals fresh from the Mass
for Electing the Pope, invoked the true architect for their very presence in the Sistine Chapel. What followed was in the hands of the
Holy Spirit. Cardinal Saraiva Martins, Prefect for the Congregation
for the Causes of Saints, perhaps had the most accurate and thought-
ful prediction of the entire week: "I think it will be short. The Holy
Spirit works quickly."

PART II

"Habemus Papam!": We Have a Pope!

Chapter 4

WHITE SMOKE AND BELLS
———————✠———————

*I announce to you with great joy: We have a Pope! The most emi-
nent and most reverend Lord, Joseph, Cardinal of the Holy
Roman Church, Ratzinger, who has taken the name Benedict
XVI!*

— CARDINAL JORGE ARTURO MEDINA ESTEVEZ,
APRIL 19, 2005

On the morning of April 18, the Cardinals gathered in St. Peter's
Basilica for the Mass for Electing the Supreme Pontiff (the
missa pro eligendo romano pontifice). In that Mass, the homily traditionally delivered by the Dean of the College of Cardinals, assumed
a sudden and heightened importance because of the speculation that
had attended the apparent push for Cardinal Ratzinger's possible
ascendancy heading into the conclave.

Indeed, Ratzinger entered the conclave the heaviest favorite in
four decades and the most internationally well-known member of the
Sacred College since 1939. In 1939, as the planet lurched toward
World War II, the Cardinals who had gathered to choose a successor
to Pope Pius XI recognized that the global situation required the
steady hand of a diplomat and Cardinal best suited to deal with the
impending disaster of war. They chose Cardinal Eugenio Pacelli, the
brilliant papal diplomat and Cardinal Secretary of State who had
been nuncio to Germany and was perfectly prepared to assume the
papacy under such difficult circumstances. In 1963, the Cardinals
electing a successor to Pope John XXIII opted for the favorite Cardinal Giovanni Battista Montini, the Archbishop of Milan and a

long-time Vatican figure who had been one of the architects for Pope John of the Second Vatican Council. The conclave that gathered in the Sistine Chapel elected him Pope Paul VI.

In the Mass for Electing the Pope, Cardinal Ratzinger spoke eloquently but forthrightly about what he saw facing the Church.

> How many winds of doctrine have we known in recent decades, how many ideological currents, how many ways of thinking. The small boat of the thought of many Christians has often been tossed about by these waves — flung from one extreme to another: from Marxism to liberalism, even to libertinism; from collectivism to radical individualism; from atheism to a vague religious mysticism; from agnosticism to syncretism and so forth. Every day new sects spring up, and what St. Paul says about human deception and the trickery that strives to entice people into error (cf. Eph 4: 14) comes true.
>
> Today, having a clear faith based on the Creed of the Church is often labeled as fundamentalism. Whereas relativism, that is, letting oneself be "tossed here and there, carried about by every wind of doctrine," seems the only attitude that can cope with modern times. We are building a dictatorship of relativism that does not recognize anything as definitive and whose ultimate goal consists solely of one's own ego and desires.

Contrary to the media reaction — which described the homily as dour, dire, grim, and reactionary — the Dean was eloquent in speaking directly to the challenges of the Church at the start of the millennium, and he was in clear fidelity to the topics discussed at the Synods and consistories of the previous five years. He finished with a telling comment:

> The fruit that endures is therefore all that we have sown in human souls: love, knowledge, a gesture capable of touching hearts, words that open the soul to joy in the Lord. So let us go and pray to the Lord to help us bear fruit that endures. Only

in this way will the earth be changed from a valley of tears to a garden of God.

The precise dynamics of the election and the internal discussions and actual voting in the conclave that followed over the next day will be pieced together by Church historians, writers, and journalists for decades to come. For the rest of the world, what was seen in the unprecedented television coverage of the procession told a tale of antiquity, profound spirituality, and the awesome and terrible duty placed upon the Cardinals as they took their oath upon the Gospels before an audience of over one billion people. The proceedings were then shrouded in the time-honored secrecy of the conclave. There remained only to wait for the verdict of the Holy Spirit.

The television cameras pointed toward the chimneystack protruding from the Sistine Chapel and simply awaited the smoke. It took only one day after the doors of the Chapel were closed for smoke to rise at 5:50 p.m., after the fourth ballot of the conclave, one of the shortest in the previous hundred years (only the conclave of 1939 was faster). The crowds gathered in the Square were at first uncertain that white smoke was billowing, and thoughts went to 1978 when confusion reigned temporarily as to whether a new Pope had been chosen. The white smoke kept coming, however, and the eyes of the crowd and the vast television and radio audiences turned to the bell of St. Peter's Basilica and waited with anticipation for the telltale ringing that was supposed to follow the smoke. After what seemed an eternity, the bells began toll — the smoke had been white, and the conclave was over.

From all over the city, Italians, tourists, nuns, priests, seminarians, the old and the young, poured through the pillars of the Bernini's Colonnade that stretches like two arms around the Square. Within minutes, there were some 200,000 in attendance steadily watching the red curtain on the central window of the loggia for the announcement.

Finally, the curtain parted, and Cardinal Jorge Medina Estevez, Senior Cardinal Deacon, proceeded to the balustrade and made the announcement in Latin: *"Habemus papam!"* The frenzied crowd did not lessen in its enthusiasm when he began the lengthy announcement of the Cardinal's name and it was apparent immediately that Joseph Aloysius Ratzinger had been elected and had taken the name Benedict XVI.

The new Pope walked with determination and genuine elation onto the loggia of the basilica, and the world at large was for the first

THE CHOICE OF A NAME

"I wish to speak of the name I chose on becoming bishop of Rome and pastor of the universal Church. I chose to call myself Benedict XVI ideally as a link to the venerated Pontiff, Benedict XV, who guided the Church through the turbulent times of the First World War. He was a true and courageous prophet of peace who struggled strenuously and bravely, first to avoid the drama of war and then to limit its terrible consequences. In his footsteps I place my ministry, in the service of reconciliation and harmony between peoples, profoundly convinced that the great good of peace is above all a gift of God, a fragile and precious gift to be invoked, safeguarded, and constructed, day after day and with everyone's contribution.

"The name Benedict also evokes the extraordinary figure of the great 'patriarch of western monasticism,' St. Benedict of Nursia, co-patron of Europe with Cyril and Methodius. The progressive expansion of the Benedictine Order which he founded exercised an enormous influence on the spread of Christianity throughout the European continent. For this reason, St. Benedict is much venerated in Germany, and especially in Bavaria, my own land of origin; he constitutes a fundamental point of reference for the unity of Europe and a powerful call to the irrefutable Christian roots of European culture and civilization.

"I ask him to help us all to hold firm to the centrality of Christ in our Christian life: May Christ always take first place in our thoughts and actions!"

— POPE BENEDICT XVI, GENERAL AUDIENCE, APRIL 27, 2005

POPE BENEDICT XVI

L'OSSERVATORE ROMANO PHOTO

Joseph Ratzinger as a young scholar (undated photo)

CNS PHOTO FROM CATHOLIC PRESS PHOTO

Archbishop Joseph Ratzinger in 1977

© BETTMANN/CORBIS

Cardinal Joseph Ratzinger in Rome (1985)

© GIANNI GIANSANTI/SYGMA/CORBIS

Cardinal Ratzinger washing the feet of a priest during Holy Thursday Mass in St. Peter's Basilica (2004)

L'OSSERVATORE ROMANO PHOTO

Cardinal Ratzinger censing the coffin of Pope John Paul II at the funeral Mass

© GIAMPIERO SPOSITO/REUTERS/CORBIS

Papal portrait (April 19, 2005)

L'OSSERVATORE ROMANO PHOTO

Pope Benedict XVI's first appearance

Waving to a packed St. Peter's Square

L'OSSERVATORE ROMANO PHOTO

L'OSSERVATORE ROMANO PHOTO

L'OSSERVATORE ROMANO PHOTO

L'OSSERVATORE ROMANO PHOTO

L'Osservatore Romano photo

Pope Benedict entering Torre San Giovanni on the Vatican grounds (April 20, 2005)

L'OSSERVATORE ROMANO PHOTO

CNS PHOTO FROM CATHOLIC PRESS PHOTO

Greeting a crowd outside his former residence

PHOTO BY GRZEGORZ GALAZKA

Pope Benedict XVI kissing the altar at beginning of installation Mass (April 24, 2005)

Receiving the pallium

Photo by Grzegorz Galazka

Receiving the papal ring

Photo by Grzegorz Galazka

time meeting the man, the priest, the bishop, the Cardinal, and now the Pope who was so well-known, respected, and even loved by those who know him best and with whom he has worked for so long for the Church. Known always as a retiring, even shy figure, the new pontiff struggled slightly with the sudden glare of being at the world's center of attention. The new Pope Benedict XVI greeted the crowd in fluent Italian and began his pontificate with words of humility, warmth, and gratitude:

Dear Brothers and Sisters,

After the great Pope John Paul II, the Cardinals have elected me, a simple and humble laborer in the vineyard of the Lord.

The fact that the Lord knows how to work and to act even with inadequate instruments comforts me, and above all I entrust myself to your prayers.

Let us move forward in the joy of the Risen Lord, confident of His unfailing help! The Lord will help us, and Mary, His Most Holy Mother, will be on our side. Thank you.

The Cardinals and the Holy Spirit had spoken. The speed of the conclave was a testament that the 115 Cardinal Electors reached a swift consensus that Joseph Ratzinger was the one person in whom they could put their trust and the well-being of over one billion Catholic souls. As American Cardinal Francis George put it right after the conclave ended, "It was a choice that was clear almost from the beginning," and another American, Cardinal Theodore McCarrick, added, "Obviously he realized that he was going to be someone that obviously we would look at because of his tremendous experience and because of his holiness and because we've all gotten to know him over the years. I was not surprised when the Holy Spirit told us to choose Cardinal Ratzinger, I'm sure no one was."

The man the Cardinals had chosen was more than the Dean of the College of Cardinals and a prominent figure in the Curia in Rome. Joseph Ratzinger was one of the foremost theologians of the

German Popes

Gregory V: Saxony, 996-999

Clement II: Saxony, 1046-1047

Damasus II: Bavaria, 1048

St. Leo IX: Alsace, 1049-1054

Victor II: Swabia, 1055-1057

Benedict XVI: Bavaria, 2005-Present

20th century, and one of the most determined champions of the legacy of John Paul II. The message from the College of Cardinals was clear: the papacy was entrusted not to some caretaker pontiff. That Joseph Ratzinger was the oldest Cardinal elected since 1730 and Pope Clement XII was irrelevant. Rather, the College of Cardinals was insuring the continuity of John Paul's rich pontificate and insuring as well that the next years would witness the advance of those ideas united with the vision of a gentle, humble, determined, and eloquent pontiff.

The election of Benedict XVI marked the most dramatic call as well by the Cardinals for fidelity to the Second Vatican Council — of which Joseph Ratzinger was a truly prominent member — and hence for fidelity to the task of the Church for 2,000 years to proclaim the Gospel in every corner of the world.

Far from Rome and the jubilation of the crowds, the cheers of the young nuns and especially the seminarians from all over the globe who were studying in Rome, bells greeted the announcement in several small towns in Bavaria. In the picturesque village of Marktl am Inn, the residents exploded with delight that a native son had been elected Pope. In Traunstein, the reaction was similar, marked by the tolling of the bell in the church of St. Oswald's in the hamlet of Hufschlag. There, on the morning of July, 1951, a young newly ordained priest of twenty-four had celebrated Mass for the first time. Fifty-four years later, that young man stood upon the loggia of St. Peter's Basilica as Benedict XVI.

Chapter 5

SERVANT OF THE SERVANTS
OF GOD

✠

In Te, Domine, speravi; non confundar in aeternum! ("O Lord,
in Thee I have put my trust; let me never be put to shame!")

— FROM THE TRADITIONAL PRAYER THE *TE DEUM*

On April 20, 2005, Pope Benedict XVI celebrated Mass with the
members of the College of Cardinals in the Sistine Chapel,
where he had been elected Supreme Pontiff barely twelve hours
before. The homily took on considerable importance as it was the
first official address by the Pope after the brief *Urbi et Orbi* benedic-
tion he had delivered on the loggia of St. Peter's Basilica.

Pope Benedict spoke directly to the Cardinals as his collaborators, pledging to follow the path laid out by Pope John Paul II in
striving for dialogue with all, including those of other religions and
"various civilizations" to bring "mutual understanding" and "a better
future for everyone." For Benedict, the Second Vatican Council
remains essential for the future life of the Church, as the teachings in
the conciliar documents "have shown themselves to be especially
pertinent to the new exigencies of the Church and the present globalized society." He also provided a detailed presentation on the
Eucharist, "the heart of Christian life," and called especially on young
people in anticipation of his visit with them in Cologne during the
2005 World Youth Day.

While not stating a formal program for the coming years, the
new Pope in this first address developed several major themes that

have since become cornerstones for the first days of his pontificate. Below is the complete text of the homily:

"Grace and peace in abundance to all of you! In my soul there are two contrasting sentiments in these hours. On the one hand, a sense of inadequacy and human turmoil for the responsibility entrusted to me yesterday as the Successor of the Apostle Peter in this See of Rome, with regard to the Universal Church. On the other hand I sense within me profound gratitude to God Who — as the liturgy makes us sing — does not abandon His flock, but leads it throughout time, under the guidance of those whom He has chosen as vicars of His Son, and made pastors.

"Dear Ones, this intimate recognition for a gift of divine mercy prevails in my heart in spite of everything. I consider this a grace obtained for me by my venerated predecessor, John Paul II. It seems I can feel his strong hand squeezing mine; I seem to see his smiling eyes and listen to his words, addressed to me especially at this moment: 'Do not be afraid!'

> ✠
>
> *And it is to Christ in the first place that I renew my total and trustworthy adhesion:* "In Te, Domine, speravi; non confundar in aeternum!"

"The death of the Holy Father John Paul II, and the days which followed, were for the Church and for the entire world an extraordinary time of grace. The great pain for his death and the void that it left in all of us were tempered by the action of the Risen Christ, which showed itself during long days in the choral wave of faith, love and spiritual solidarity, culminating in his solemn funeral.

"We can say it: the funeral of John Paul II was a truly extraordinary experience in which was perceived in some way the power of God Who, through His Church, wishes to form a great family of all peoples, through the unifying force of Truth and Love. In the hour of death, conformed to his Master and Lord, John Paul II crowned his long and fruitful pontificate, confirming the Christian people in faith, gathering them around him and making the entire human family feel more united.

"How can one not feel sustained by this witness? How can one not feel the encouragement that comes from this event of grace?

"Surprising every prevision I had, Divine Providence, through the will of the venerable Cardinal Fathers, called me to succeed this great Pope. I have been thinking in these hours about what happened in the region of Cesarea of Phillippi two thousand years ago: I seem to hear the words of Peter: 'You are Christ, the Son of the living God,' and the solemn affirmation of the Lord: 'You are Peter and on this rock I will build my Church . . . I will give you the keys of the kingdom of heaven.'

"You are Christ! You are Peter! It seems I am reliving this very Gospel scene; I, the Successor of Peter, repeat with trepidation the anxious words of the fisherman from Galilee and I listen again with intimate emotion to the reassuring promise of the divine Master. If the weight of the responsibility that now lies on my poor shoulders is enormous, the divine power on which I can count is surely immeasurable: 'You are Peter and on this rock I will build my Church.' Electing me as the Bishop of Rome, the Lord wanted me as his Vicar, he wished me to be the 'rock' upon which everyone may rest with confidence. I ask him to make up for the poverty of my strength, that I may be a courageous and faithful pastor of His flock, always docile to the inspirations of His Spirit.

"I undertake this special ministry, the 'Petrine' ministry at the service of the Universal Church, with humble abandon to the hands of the Providence of God. And it is to Christ in the first place that I renew my total and trustworthy adhesion: *'In Te, Domine, speravi; non confundar in aeternum!'*

"To you, Lord Cardinals, with a grateful soul for the trust shown me, I ask you to sustain me with prayer and with constant, active and wise collaboration. I also ask my brothers in the episcopacy to be close to me in prayer and counsel so that I may truly be the *'Servus servorum Dei'* (Servant of the servants of God). As Peter and the other

Apostles were, through the will of the Lord, one apostolic college, in the same way the Successor of Peter and the Bishops, successors of the Apostles — and the Council forcefully repeated this — must be closely united among themselves. This collegial communion, even in the diversity of roles and functions of the Supreme Pontiff and the bishops, is at the service of the Church and the unity of faith, from which depend in a notable measure the effectiveness of the evangelizing action of the contemporary world. Thus, this path, upon which my venerated predecessors went forward, I too intend to follow, concerned solely with proclaiming to the world the living presence of Christ.

"Before my eyes is, in particular, the witness of Pope John Paul II. He leaves us a Church that is more courageous, freer, younger. A Church that, according to his teaching and example, looks with serenity to the past and is not afraid of the future. With the Great Jubilee the Church was introduced into the new millennium carrying in her hands the Gospel, applied to the world through the authoritative rereading of Vatican Council II. Pope John Paul II justly indicated the Council as a 'compass' with which to orient ourselves in the vast ocean of the third millennium. Also in his spiritual testament he noted: 'I am convinced that for a very long time the new generations will draw upon the riches that this council of the 20th century gave us.'

"I too, as I start in the service that is proper to the Successor of Peter, wish to affirm with force my decided will to pursue the commitment to enact Vatican Council II, in the wake of my predecessors and in faithful continuity with the millennia-old tradition of the Church. Precisely this year is the 40th anniversary of the conclusion of this conciliar assembly (December 8, 1965). With the passing of time, the conciliar documents have not lost their timeliness; their teachings have shown themselves to be especially pertinent to the new exigencies of the Church and the present globalized society.

"In a very significant way, my pontificate starts as the Church is living the special year dedicated to the Eucharist. How can I not see in this providential coincidence an element that must mark the ministry to which I have been called? The Eucharist, the heart of Christian life and the source of the evangelizing mission of the Church, cannot but be the permanent center and the source of the petrine service entrusted to me.

"The Eucharist makes the Risen Christ constantly present, Christ Who continues to give Himself to us, calling us to participate in the banquet of His Body and His Blood. From this full communion with Him comes every other element of the life of the Church, in the first place the communion among the faithful, the commitment to proclaim and give witness to the Gospel, the ardor of charity towards all, especially towards the poor and the smallest.

> *Theological dialogue is necessary. A profound examination of the historical reasons behind past choices is also indispensable.*

"In this year, therefore, the Solemnity of Corpus Christi must be celebrated in a particularly special way. The Eucharist will be at the center, in August, of World Youth Day in Cologne and, in October, of the ordinary Assembly of the Synod of Bishops which will take place on the theme "The Eucharist, Source and Summit of the Life and Mission of the Church.' I ask everyone to intensify in coming months love and devotion to the Eucharistic Jesus and to express in a courageous and clear way the real presence of the Lord, above all through the solemnity and the correctness of the celebrations.

"I ask this in a special way of priests, about whom I am thinking in this moment with great affection. The priestly ministry was born in the Cenacle, together with the Eucharist, as my venerated predecessor John Paul II underlined so many times. 'The priestly life must have in a special way a 'Eucharistic form,' he wrote in his last Letter for Holy Thursday. The devout daily celebration of Holy Mass, the center of the life and mission of every priest, contributes to this end.

"Nourished and sustained by the Eucharist, Catholics cannot but feel stimulated to tend towards that full unity for which Christ hoped in the Cenacle. Peter's Successor knows that he must take on this supreme desire of the Divine Master in a particularly special way. To him, indeed, has been entrusted the duty of strengthening his brethren.

"Thus, in full awareness and at the beginning of his ministry in the Church of Rome that Peter bathed with his blood, the current Successor assumes as his primary commitment that of working tirelessly towards the reconstitution of the full and visible unity of all Christ's followers. This is his ambition, this is his compelling duty. He is aware that to do so, expressions of good feelings are not enough. Concrete gestures are required to penetrate souls and move consciences, encouraging everyone to that interior conversion which is the basis for all progress on the road of ecumenism.

"Theological dialogue is necessary. A profound examination of the historical reasons behind past choices is also indispensable. But even more urgent is that 'purification of memory,' which was so often evoked by John Paul II, and which alone can dispose souls to welcome the full truth of Christ. It is before Him, supreme Judge of all living things, that each of us must stand, in the awareness that one day we must explain to Him what we did and what we did not do for the great good that is the full and visible unity of all His disciples.

> *Stay with us Lord! This invocation, which forms the dominant theme of John Paul II's Apostolic Letter for the Year of the Eucharist, is the prayer that comes spontaneously from my heart as I turn to begin the ministry to which Christ has called me.*

"The current Successor of Peter feels himself to be personally implicated in this question and is disposed to do all in his power to promote the fundamental cause of ecumenism. In the wake of his predecessors, he is fully determined to cultivate any initiative that may seem appropriate to promote contact and agreement with representatives from the various Churches and ecclesial communities.

Indeed, on this occasion too, he sends them his most cordial greetings in Christ, the one Lord of all.

"In this moment, I go back in my memory to the unforgettable experience we all underwent with the death and the funeral of the lamented John Paul II. Around his mortal remains, lying on the bare earth, leaders of nations gathered, with people from all social classes and especially the young, in an unforgettable embrace of affection and admiration. The entire world looked to him with trust. To many it seemed as if that intense participation, amplified to the confines of the planet by the social communications media, was like a choral request for help addressed to the Pope by modern humanity which, wracked by fear and uncertainty, questions itself about the future.

"The Church today must revive within herself an awareness of the task to present the world again with the voice of the One Who said: 'I am the light of the world; he who follows me will not walk in darkness but will have the light of life.' In undertaking his ministry, the new Pope knows that his task is to bring the light of Christ to shine before the men and women of today: not his own light but that of Christ.

"With this awareness, I address myself to everyone, even to those who follow other religions or who are simply seeking an answer to the fundamental questions of life and have not yet found it. I address everyone with simplicity and affection, to assure them that the Church wants to continue to build an open and sincere dialogue with them, in a search for the true good of mankind and of society.

"From God I invoke unity and peace for the human family and declare the willingness of all Catholics to cooperate for true social development, one that respects the dignity of all human beings.

"I will make every effort and dedicate myself to pursuing the promising dialogue that my predecessors began with various civilizations, because it is mutual understanding that gives rise to conditions for a better future for everyone.

"I am particularly thinking of young people. To them, the privileged interlocutors of John Paul II, I send an affectionate embrace in the hope, God willing, of meeting them at Cologne on the occasion of the next World Youth Day. With you, dear young people, I will continue to maintain a dialogue, listening to your expectations in an attempt to help you meet ever more profoundly the living, ever young, Christ.

"*'Mane nobiscum, Domine!'* Stay with us Lord! This invocation, which forms the dominant theme of John Paul II's Apostolic Letter for the Year of the Eucharist, is the prayer that comes spontaneously from my heart as I turn to begin the ministry to which Christ has called me. Like Peter, I too renew to Him my unconditional promise of faithfulness. He alone I intend to serve as I dedicate myself totally to the service of His Church.

"In support of this promise, I invoke the maternal intercession of Mary Most Holy, in whose hands I place the present and the future of my person and of the Church. May the Holy Apostles Peter and Paul, and all the saints, also intercede.

"With these sentiments I impart to you venerated brother Cardinals, to those participating in this ritual, and to all those following to us by television and radio, a special and affectionate blessing."

Chapter 6

THE PALLIUM AND THE FISHERMAN'S RING

✠

*He said to him the third time, "Simon, son of John, do you love
me?" Peter was grieved because he said to him the third time, "Do
you love me?" And he said to him, "Lord, you know everything;
you know that I love you." Jesus said to him, "Feed my sheep."*

— JOHN 21:17

On April 24, 2005, Pope Benedict XVI was formally installed as
Supreme Pontiff of the Church at an outdoor Mass in St.
Peter's Square. The Mass was attended by some 500,000 people,
including a host of dignitaries from around the world. The United
States was represented by Jeb Bush, governor of Florida and brother
of President George W. Bush; German Chancellor Gerhard
Schroeder; Dr. Rowan Williams, the Archbishop of Canterbury and
head of the Anglican Communion; and numerous representatives of
the Orthodox Churches and other denominations and religions.

Pope Benedict's homily revealed his strengths as a theologian, but
it also demonstrated his deep pastoral qualities and more so his qualities as a teacher. Once again, as in his address to the Cardinals in the
Sistine Chapel, the new Pope declined to present a formal program
for the Church. Rather, he spoke from the heart to the faithful in
attendance and the massive television audience around the world, cit-
ing his own weakness in assuming the terrible burdens of the papacy
and the fact that he could not bear such a weight without the confi-

dence of knowing that he is not alone. As he put it, "Those who believe are never alone — neither in life nor in death."

Rather than addressing the direction of his pontificate, Pope Benedict declared that his "real program of governance" will be in listening with the entire Church "to the word and the will of the Lord." Pope Benedict is one of the foremost theologians of the modern age, but he reminded the Church that he was also one of the great teachers. His homily was a teaching moment and discussed the many layers of meaning behind the use of the pallium and the Ring of the Fisherman. The pastoral strength of the homily set the tone for the start of a papacy that was immediately obvious in its pastoral orientation and its constant urging of unity and dialogue rooted in charity.

His entire homily follows.

"Your Eminences, my dear brother bishops and priests, distinguished authorities and members of the diplomatic corps, dear brothers and sisters.

"During these days of great intensity, we have chanted the litany of the saints on three different occasions: at the funeral of our Holy Father John Paul II; as the Cardinals entered the conclave; and again today, when we sang it with the response: '*Tu illum adiuva*' — sustain the new Successor of Saint Peter. On each occasion, in a particular way, I found great consolation in listening to this prayerful chant. How alone we all felt after the passing of John Paul II — the Pope who for over twenty-six years had been our shepherd and guide on our journey through life! He crossed the threshold of the next life, entering into the mystery of God. But he did not take this step alone. Those who believe are never alone — neither in life nor in death. At that moment, we could call upon the saints from every age — his friends, his brothers and sisters in the faith — knowing that they would form a living procession to accompany him into the next world, into the glory of God. We knew that his arrival was awaited. Now we know that he is among his own and is truly at home.

"We were also consoled as we made our solemn entrance into conclave, to elect the one whom the Lord had chosen. How would we be able to discern his name? How could 115 bishops, from every culture and every country, discover the one on whom the Lord wished to confer the mission of binding and loosing? Once again, we knew that we were not alone, we knew that we were surrounded, led and guided by the friends of God. And now, at this moment, weak servant of God that I am, I must assume this enormous task, which truly exceeds all human capacity. How can I do this? How will I be able to do it? All of you, my dear friends, have just invoked the entire host of saints, represented by some of the great names in the history of God's dealings with mankind. In this way, I too can say with renewed conviction: I am not alone. I do not have to carry alone what in truth I could never carry alone. All the saints of God are there to protect me, to sustain me and to carry me. And your prayers, my dear friends, your indulgence, your love, your faith and your hope accompany me. Indeed, the communion of saints consists not only of the great men and women who went before us and whose names we know. All of us belong to the communion of saints, we who have been baptized in the name of the Father, and of the Son and of the Holy Spirit, we who draw life from the gift of Christ's Body and Blood, through which He transforms us and makes us like Himself.

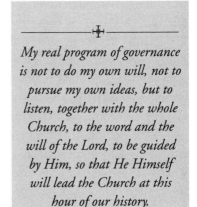

My real program of governance is not to do my own will, not to pursue my own ideas, but to listen, together with the whole Church, to the word and the will of the Lord, to be guided by Him, so that He Himself will lead the Church at this hour of our history.

"Yes, the Church is alive — this is the wonderful experience of these days. During those sad days of the Pope's illness and death, it became wonderfully evident to us that the Church is alive. And the Church is young. She holds within herself the future of the world and therefore shows each of us the way towards the future. The Church is alive and we are seeing it: we are experiencing the joy that the Risen Lord promised His followers. The Church is alive — she is alive because Christ is alive, because He is truly risen. In the suffering that we saw on the Holy Father's face in those days of Easter, we contemplated the mystery of Christ's Passion and we touched His wounds. But throughout these days we have also been able, in a profound sense, to touch the Risen One. We have been able to experience the joy that He promised, after a brief period of darkness, as the fruit of His resurrection.

"The Church is alive — with these words, I greet with great joy and gratitude all of you gathered here, my venerable brother Cardinals and bishops, my dear priests, deacons, Church workers, catechists. I greet you, men and women religious, witnesses of the transfiguring presence of God. I greet you, members of the lay faithful, immersed in the great task of building up the Kingdom of God which spreads throughout the world, in every area of life. With great affection I also greet all those who have been reborn in the sacrament of baptism but are not yet in full communion with us; and you, my brothers and sisters of the Jewish people, to whom we are joined by a great shared spiritual heritage, one rooted in God's irrevocable promises. Finally, like a wave gathering force, my thoughts go out to all men and women of today, to believers and non-believers alike.

"Dear friends! At this moment there is no need for me to present a program of governance. I was able to give an indication of what I see as my task in my message of Wednesday, April 20, and there will be other opportunities to do so. My real program of governance is not to do my own will, not to pursue my own ideas, but to listen, together with the whole Church, to the word and the will of the Lord, to be guided by Him, so that He Himself will lead the Church at this hour of our history. Instead of putting forward a program, I should simply like to comment on the two liturgical symbols which represent the inauguration of the Petrine Ministry; both these symbols, moreover, reflect clearly what we heard proclaimed in today's readings.

"The first symbol is the pallium, woven in pure wool, which will be placed on my shoulders. This ancient sign, which the Bishops of Rome have worn since the 4th century, may be considered an image of the yoke of Christ, which the bishop of this city, the Servant of the Servants of God, takes upon his shoulders. God's yoke is God's will, which we accept. And this will does not weigh down on us, oppressing us and taking away our freedom. To know what God wants, to know where the path of life is found — this was Israel's joy, this was her great privilege. It is also our joy: God's will does not alienate us, it purifies us — even if this can be painful — and so it leads us to ourselves. In this way, we serve not only Him, but the salvation of the whole world, of all history.

> ✠
>
> *And yet, we need His patience. God, Who became a lamb, tells us that the world is saved by the Crucified One, not by those who crucified Him. The world is redeemed by the patience of God. It is destroyed by the impatience of man.*

"The symbolism of the pallium is even more concrete: the lamb's wool is meant to represent the lost, sick or weak sheep which the shepherd places on his shoulders and carries to the waters of life. For the Fathers of the Church, the parable of the lost sheep, which the shepherd seeks in the desert, was an image of the mystery of Christ and the Church. The human race — every one of us — is the sheep lost in the desert which no longer knows the way. The Son of God will not let this happen; He cannot abandon humanity in so wretched a condition. He leaps to his feet and abandons the glory of heaven, in order to go in search of the sheep and pursue it, all the way to the Cross. He takes it upon His shoulders and carries our humanity; He carries us all — He is the good shepherd who lays down His life for the sheep. What the pallium indicates first and foremost is that we are all carried by Christ. But at the same time it invites us to carry one another. Hence the pallium becomes a symbol of the shepherd's mission, of which the second reading and the Gospel speak. The pastor must be inspired by Christ's holy zeal: for him it is not a matter of indifference that so many people are living in the desert. And there are so many kinds of desert. There is the desert of poverty, the desert of hunger and thirst, the desert of abandonment, of loneliness, of destroyed love. There is the desert of God's darkness, the emptiness of souls no longer aware of their dignity or the goal of human life. The external deserts in the world are growing, because the internal deserts have become so vast. Therefore the earth's treasures no longer serve to build God's garden for all to live in, but they have been made to serve the powers of exploitation and destruction. The Church as a whole and all her pastors, like Christ, must set out to lead people out of the desert, towards the place of life, towards friendship with the Son of God, towards the One who gives us life, and life in abundance.

"The symbol of the lamb also has a deeper meaning. In the ancient Near East, it was customary for kings to style themselves shepherds of their people. This was an image of their power, a cynical image: to them their subjects were like sheep, which the shepherd could dispose of as he wished. When the shepherd of all humanity, the living God, Himself became a lamb, He stood on the side of the lambs, with those who are downtrodden and killed. This is how He reveals Himself to be the true shepherd: 'I am the Good Shepherd . . . I lay down my life for the sheep,' Jesus says of Himself (Jn 10:14ff). It is not power, but love that redeems us! This is God's sign: He Himself is love. How often we wish that God would make show Himself stronger, that He would strike decisively, defeating evil and creating a better world. All ideologies of power justify themselves in exactly this way, they justify the destruction of whatever would stand in the way of progress and the liberation of humanity. We suffer on account of God's patience. And yet, we need His patience. God, Who became a lamb, tells us that the world is saved by the Crucified

One, not by those who crucified Him. The world is redeemed by the patience of God. It is destroyed by the impatience of man.

"One of the basic characteristics of a shepherd must be to love the people entrusted to him, even as he loves Christ whom he serves. 'Feed my sheep.' says Christ to Peter, and now, at this moment, He says it to me as well. Feeding means loving, and loving also means being ready to suffer. Loving means giving the sheep what is truly good, the nourishment of God's truth, of God's word, the nourishment of His presence, which He gives us in the Blessed Sacrament. My dear friends — at this moment I can only say: pray for me, that I may learn to love the Lord more and more. Pray for me, that I may learn to love His flock more and more — in other words, you, the holy Church, each one of you and all of you together. Pray for me, that I may not flee for fear of the wolves. Let us pray for one another, that the Lord will carry us and that we will learn to carry one another.

"The second symbol used in today's liturgy to express the inauguration of the Petrine ministry is the presentation of the fisherman's ring. Peter's call to be a shepherd, which we heard in the Gospel, comes after the account of a miraculous catch of fish: after a night in which the disciples had let down their nets without success, they see the Risen Lord on the shore. He tells them to let down their nets once more, and the nets become so full that they can hardly pull them in; 153 large fish: 'and although there were so many, the net was not torn' (Jn 21:11). This account, coming at the end of Jesus' earthly journey with His disciples, corresponds to an account found at the beginning: there too, the disciples had caught nothing the entire night; there too, Jesus had invited Simon once more to put out into the deep. And Simon, who was not yet called Peter, gave the wonderful reply: 'Master, at your word I will let down the nets.' And then came the conferral of his mission: 'Do not be afraid. Henceforth you will be catching men' (Lk 5:1-11). Today too the Church and the successors of the Apostles are told to put out into the deep sea of history and to let down the nets, so as to win men and women over to the Gospel — to God, to Christ, to true life. The Fathers made a very significant commentary on this singular task. This is what they say: for a fish, created for water, it is fatal to be taken out of the sea, to be removed from its vital element to serve as human food. But in the mission of a fisher of men, the reverse is true. We are living in alienation, in the salt waters of suffering and death; in a sea of darkness without light. The net of the Gospel pulls us out of the waters of death and brings us into the splendor of God's light, into true life. It is really true: as we follow Christ in this mission to be fishers of men, we must bring men and women out of the sea that is salted with so many forms of alienation and onto the land of life, into the light of God.

> *We are living in alienation, in the salt waters of suffering and death; in a sea of darkness without light. The net of the Gospel pulls us out of the waters of death and brings us into the splendor of God's light, into true life.*

"It is really so: the purpose of our lives is to reveal God to men. And only where God is seen does life truly begin. Only when we meet the living God in Christ do we know what life is. We are not some casual and meaningless product of evolution. Each of us is the result of a thought of God. Each of us is willed, each of us is loved, each of us is necessary. There is nothing more beautiful than to be surprised by the Gospel, by the encounter with Christ. There is nothing more beautiful than to know Him and to speak to others of our friendship with Him. The task of the shepherd, the task of the fisher of men, can often seem wearisome. But it is beautiful and wonderful, because it is truly a service to joy, to God's joy which longs to break into the world.

"Here I want to add something: both the image of the shepherd and that of the fisherman issue an explicit call to unity. 'I have other sheep that are not of this fold; I must lead them too, and they will heed my voice. So there shall be one flock, one shepherd' (Jn 10:16); these are the words of Jesus at the end of His discourse on the Good

Shepherd. And the account of the 153 large fish ends with the joyful statement: 'although there were so many, the net was not torn' (Jn 21:11). Alas, beloved Lord, with sorrow we must now acknowledge that it has been torn! But no — we must not be sad! Let us rejoice because of Your promise, which does not disappoint, and let us do all we can to pursue the path towards the unity You have promised. Let us remember it in our prayer to the Lord, as we plead with Him: yes, Lord, remember Your promise. Grant that we may be one flock and one shepherd! Do not allow Your net to be torn, help us to be servants of unity!

"At this point, my mind goes back to October 22, 1978, when Pope John Paul II began his ministry here in Saint Peter's Square. His words on that occasion constantly echo in my ears: 'Do not be afraid! Open wide the doors for Christ!' The Pope was addressing the mighty, the powerful of this world, who feared that Christ might take away something of their power if they were to let Him in, if they were to allow the faith to be free. Yes, He would certainly have taken something away from them: the dominion of corruption, the manipulation of law and the freedom to do as they pleased. But He would not have taken away anything that pertains to human freedom or dignity, or to the building of a just society. The Pope was also speaking to everyone, especially the young. Are we not perhaps all afraid in some way? If we let Christ enter fully into our lives, if we open ourselves totally to Him, are we not afraid that He might take something away from us? Are we not perhaps afraid to give up something significant, something unique, something that makes life so beautiful? Do we not then risk ending up diminished and deprived of our freedom? And once again the Pope said: No! If we let Christ into our lives, we lose nothing, nothing, absolutely nothing of what makes life free, beautiful and great. No! Only in this friendship are the doors of life opened wide. Only in this friendship is the great potential of human existence truly revealed. Only in this friendship do we experience beauty and liberation. And so, today, with great strength and great conviction, on the basis of long personal experience of life, I say to you, dear young people: Do not be afraid of Christ! He takes nothing away, and He gives you everything. When we give ourselves to Him, we receive a hundredfold in return. Yes, open, open wide the doors to Christ — and you will find true life. Amen."

PART III

---✝---

"Tu Es Petrus": You Are Peter

Chapter 7

SON OF BAVARIA

———— ✠ ————

When the pagans endeavored to force you into an idolatrous worship, you replied in the fullness of your faith that you would rather die than violate that faith in Christ which you had once for all received; filled with all joy . . .

— POPE LEO XIII, *ON THE CHURCH IN BAVARIA*

Holy Saturday 1927

The southern region of Germany, Bavaria, is one of the most picturesque anywhere in the world. Dominated by green rolling hills and towering snow-capped mountains, the region has long been blessed by two fortuitous attributes. The first is the quiet pastoral life that developed there — even if its history has at times been troubled and bloody — with picturesque villages and towns nestled beneath the mountains and in valleys that are lush in the warmer months and stunning alpine vistas in the winter months. Especially noticeable in the villages and towns are the many churches, with their distinctive bell towers, as symbols of local faith. For the Bavarians have also been known for their commitment to the Catholic Church, staying firmly devoted to the papacy even in the face of the terrible wars and upheaval that accompanied the Protestant Reformation. Through the efforts of the Holy Roman Emperors and local rulers, in particular the House of Wittelsbach, who remained determined supporters of the Catholic cause during the bleak wars of the Reformation, including the savage Thirty Years War (1618-1648), Bavaria itself remained Catholic and became a cradle of sorts for the most ornate expressions of the Catholic Reform in the late 16th and early 17th centuries. Today, Baroque monasteries such as Ettal and the church decorations encouraged by the Hapsburg rulers of the Holy Roman Empire attest to the most enthusiastic expressions of the renewed Catholic fervor in the decades after the Council of Trent ended its long deliberations in the mid-16th century. The Catholicity of Bavaria is deep, cultural, and tangible.

By the early 20th century, eastern Bavaria was still a place of villages and ornate churches. It was especially a place for a vibrant but conservative Catholic faith. The Ratzinger family had long lived in Bavaria and the roots of the family had sunk deep into the Catholic soil. Georg Ratzinger, for example, who would become the future Pope's great-uncle, was a respected writer and political figure in Bavaria during the end of the 19th century. Georg's nephew, Joseph, grew up in Bavaria and in the faith, and came from the part of the family that had been farmers from Lower Bavaria. Joseph chose not to be a farmer and served instead as a country police official and Gendarmerie-Kommissar (a local police official) living a modest lower middle-class existence. He married a woman named Maria who worked as a cook in various local hotels, and together they had three children: Maria (born in 1921), Georg (born in 1924), and a third child, a son, whom they named Joseph.

Joseph Aloysius Ratzinger was born on April 16, 1927 while the family was living in a three-story house in the little village of Marktl am Inn, in Bavaria. The newest arrival was born very early in the morning on Holy Saturday and the feast day of Benedict Joseph Labré, a pilgrim and recluse who had earned the nickname "the Beggar of Rome" before his death in 1783 and who had been canonized in 1883 by Pope Leo XIII.

From his earliest experiences, young Joseph Aloysius was surrounded by the Catholic faith. His father attended Masses and devotions with great zeal, and from his parents he learned, as he wrote in later memoirs, a critical mind (from his father) and a warm-heart and religious sense (from his mother). His father also imparted important lessons in moral courage and perseverance as the family faced the increasingly desperate conditions of Germany after the First World War.

In the wake of the Treaty of Versailles in 1919 that certified the defeat of Germany in World War I, the country was crippled by unprecedented political upheaval. The Kaiser had been deposed after the war, and the Weimar Republic proved an ineffective instrument to insure a stable democracy in a Germany plagued by partisan political warfare in the streets between communists and ardent National Socialists, by economic collapse and staggering unemployment, and feelings of despair for the future. Joseph the elder suffered from this uncertain time by having to move the family several times over the next years, starting in 1929 when they settled in Tittmoning, a small town on the Salzach River on the Austrian border. Here young Joseph spent the early days of his youth playing in the town, praying in the Ponlach Chapel, and enjoying especially the nativity scenes on display in people's houses.

By 1932, however, the elder Joseph was encountering the rising political party of the National Socialists, the Nazis, in Bavaria and was finding his position increasingly rendered impossible owing to his vocal dislike and opposition to them. So, in 1932, the Ratzingers moved to the smaller but extremely picturesque village of Aschau-am-Inn, near the tranquil Bavarian lake of Chiemsee. The young Joseph enjoyed swimming in a pond (he almost drowned there one day), but above all it was here at the base of the Alps that he first became aware of and then fell deeply in love with the Mass, receiving his first, albeit rudimentary exposure to Church Latin and also to liturgy. The family prayed the rosary and went to Mass every day, and young Joseph became used to the Church's cycle of liturgical seasons through the year that was especially heightened in the structured Catholic culture of Bavaria.

Five years later, the family moved again, this time to the hamlet of Hufschlag just outside the town of Traunstein. There they settled into a farmhouse with an attached barn and woods sprawling past the yard that Joseph the elder had purchased in 1933. As he had reached age sixty and was eligible for a pension, he retired. For young Joseph, the move meant a new school, and he spent the next two years attending the local gymnasium in Traunstein. There he received a thorough introduction to classical education, including Greek and Latin as well as music lessons that fostered in him both a skill at playing the piano and a love for Wolfgang Amadeus Mozart that has continued until today. For Joseph, Traunstein became the home of his heart and the place that he always remembered from his youth. It was a happy time and an important one as he matured in the faith.

In 1939, young Joseph made the decision with the support of his family to enter the minor seminary of Traunstein and so begin studies for the priesthood. He followed his brother Georg into the seminary he had entered several years before.

The Nazi Dictatorship

Events in Germany, however, soon intruded on his preparations for the future. In 1933, Adolf Hitler had become Chancellor of Germany and ushered in the era of Nazi domination and dictatorship. War followed in 1939 with the Nazi invasion of Poland, and by 1942, the war effort had cost Germany so many casualties that all available facilities were requisitioned. That meant the minor seminary was taken over by the German army as a military hospital. Georg found himself drafted into the *Wehrmacht* (the German Army) and Joseph went back to attending the gymnasium. While he was given the chance to study the great writers such as Göthe and Schiller, he was also confronted on a daily basis with the horrors of the war in the form of the casualty lists appearing in the local newspaper. In 1941, his brother Georg had been forced to enroll in the Hitler Youth owing to the rule that made membership compulsory for all German youth. Joseph was also registered according to the regulations but belonged only for a brief period of time and found the mandatory service an unpleasant one. He adamantly refused — like his father and other relatives — to join or have anything to do with the Nazi Party.

In 1943, Joseph was called up for duty with his entire seminary class and ordered into an anti-aircraft unit that protected a BMW factory making aircraft engines. Due to an infected finger, however, he never learned how to fire a gun and spent his time in the unit with an unloaded gun. Thus, as he later noted in an interview with *Time Magazine*, he may have been forced into the German Army, but he was never in combat and was never really a soldier. By 1944, he had been released from his unit, returned home, and was informed that

POPE BENEDICT XVI AND NAZI GERMANY

Young Joseph Ratzinger was never a Nazi. He was only 6 years old when the Nazis came to power in Germany and Adolf Hitler became Chancellor of Germany. Joseph's father was vehemently opposed to the party and taught his children that the Nazis were evil, but the imposition of Nazi laws made it mandatory for all young people to join the Hitler Youth, the youth wing of the Nazi party which combined sports and other activities with indoctrination. Resistance would have proven disastrous to his family, so 14-year-old Joseph, who was in the seminary at the time, joined under duress. He left as soon as possible and performed those required activities reluctantly. Along with fellow seminarians, he was drafted into an anti-aircraft unit of the German army at age 16 and forced into military service as happened to thousands of other young men at the end of the war. He deserted two years later without having fired a shot.

The Anti-Defamation League U.S. National Director said on April 19, 2005: "We welcome the new Papacy of Cardinal Joseph Ratzinger. From the Jewish perspective, the fact that he comes from Europe is important, because he brings with him an understanding and memory of the painful history of Europe and of the 20th-century experience of European Jewry."

he had been re-assigned to another detachment. He was then sent to the border between Austria, Hungary, and Czechoslovakia, where he found himself performing manual labor installing tank traps.

Georg told the *London Times* in an interview that both he and Joseph were opposed to the Nazi regime, but like millions of others, they were powerless to resist. "Resistance was truly impossible," he said, "Before we were conscripted, one of our teachers said we should fight and become heroic Nazis and another told us not to worry as only one soldier in a thousand was killed. But neither of us ever used a rifle against the enemy."

For the young Joseph, several incidents from his time in the military left a powerful impression. The first came while he served in the anti-aircraft unit. The work force in the BMW plant included laborers from the nearby Dachau concentration camp. The second occurred while he was in Hungary and saw Hungarian Jews being loaded onto trains and shipped off to concentration camps and certain death.

As the war effort collapsed in 1944, Joseph was sent home. Called up yet again as the Third Reich entered its final death throes, Joseph deserted in April 1945. He was by that act an enemy of the Third Reich, and had the Gestapo caught him, he would have been executed, probably in the usual manner — by being hanged from a lamppost as a warning to others. In fact, young Joseph came close to being captured, but several sympathetic soldiers allowed him to go free, using an arm injury he had suffered to serve as a suitable excuse for his release.

After the surrender of Germany, the town was finally taken by American forces. Despite the humble quality of their house, the Ratzingers were informed that the American troops intended to use it as the local headquarters for the occupation. To the family's further shock, young Joseph was arrested by American soldiers after being identified as a member of the German army. He was forced to put back on the uniform he had hated and abandoned, then marched off to line up with the other prisoners of war in a nearby field. He spent the next five weeks in a prisoner-of-war camp until finally released on June 19, 1945, after a thorough questioning. He received a joyous welcome home, and the family then waited with great anxiety until Georg also returned home after his own mandatory military service.

The war had left Joseph with a permanent understanding of the nature of evil and the calamity faced by humanity when God was rejected. For Joseph, the horrors of the war only solidified his love and admiration for the Catholic Church, for he saw the Catholic faith as true enemy of the tyranny of Nazism. He could look with pride, for example, to the Catholic bishops of Germany who had forbidden membership in the Nazi Party; to the fiery anti-Nazi letter *Mit Brennender Sorge* ("With Burning Sorrow") that had been read from every pulpit in Germany by the command of Pope Pius XI in 1937; and to the remarkable courage of such German prelates as Michael von Faulhaber (1869-1952), a Cardinal and Archbishop of Munich who was given the Grand Cross of the Order of Merit by the West German Republic for being such an outspoken critic and opponent of the

---

May the holy time of Lent and Easter, which preaches interior renovation and penance, turn Christian eyes towards the Cross and the risen Christ; be for all of you the joyful occasion that will fill your souls with heroism, patience and victory. Then We are sure, the enemies of the Church, who think that their time has come, will see that their joy was premature, and that they may close the grave they had dug. The day will come when the Te Deum of liberation will succeed to the premature hymns of the enemies of Christ: Te Deum of triumph and joy and gratitude, as the German people return to religion, bend the knee before Christ, and arming themselves against the enemies of God, again resume the task God has laid upon them.

— Pius XI, Encyclical *Mit Brennender Sorge*
("With Burning Sorrow") March 14, 1937

Nazi regime; and to the thousand priests who died at Dachau, and the many women and men who died for the faith in concentration camps and the torture chambers of the SS and Gestapo.

He found in the ideology of Nazism (as he would the ideology of Communism) the total rejection of God as Truth. That rejection took on special meaning coming as it did at the time when Joseph was coming to understand fully the centrality of the Mass in the life of the Christian. He had watched in his beloved Bavaria as the Nazis had systematically destroyed the order and structure of daily life with the false ideology of National Socialism and had tried to replace the truth of the Mass and Catholic life with pagan rituals that rejected the faith in favor of a dehumanizing ideology. The future pontiff spoke of the Catholic Church and Nazi Germany to *Time* magazine in 1993:

> The abyss of Hitlerism could not be overlooked. Only the Christian faith had the possibility to heal these people and give a new beginning.

With the war at last over, Joseph was finally able to return to the seminary with his brother and what he hoped would be his ordination to the priesthood. He finished his preparatory studies in 1947, and in September of that year entered the *Herzogliches Georgianum*, a theological institute associated with the University of Munich that offered a highly demanding course of studies. At last, on June 29, 1951, both Joseph and his brother were ordained to the priesthood by Cardinal von Faulhaber in the Cathedral at Freising, on the Feast of Sts. Peter and Paul. He and his brother Georg then had the great pleasure of saying their first Masses on July 8, in the hamlet of Hufschlag in the small but beautiful church of St. Oswald's. Father Joseph Ratzinger's first homily was on the duties given to him by Cardinal von Faulhaber and on the centrality of the Eucharist. The flock gathered in the Church sang a *Te Deum* at the end of the Mass, and a party was thrown later that day in a local restaurant.

The newly ordained Father Ratzinger was immediately assigned in August to the post of assistant pastor in the Precious Blood parish in Munich. Here he was able to develop an understanding of the pastoral care of the members of the parish and found the pastor, Father Blumschein, to be an exemplary model of the priesthood. He was also quickly overwhelmed by the extent of his duties as a young priest, but he learned within a short time that he was not destined to remain in a parish.

Having demonstrated a genuine brilliance in his studies, newly ordained Father Ratzinger was encouraged to continue his theological studies at the University of Munich. He focused his attention on the theology of St. Augustine and produced a study of the famed Church Father, *Volk und Haus Gottes in Augustins Lehre von der Kirche* ("The People and House of God in Augustine's Doctrine of the Church") that won a prize in a competition held by the university faculty and was considered worthy as a doctoral dissertation. Thus, in July 1953, he received his doctorate in theology. The dissertation itself was a reflection of the young theologian's deep respect for the teachings of St. Augustine, one that has endured throughout his life. As he declared of the great Doctor of the Church in 2004 during a Mass celebrating the 1,650th anniversary of his birth:

> Augustine experienced freedom profoundly to the point that he became its slave, as the prodigal son, who ended up by taking care of pigs and eating pods. If we are honest with ourselves, we cannot deny that that parable fully reflects our existential condition. Authentic freedom lies only in friendship with the Lord ... Words like eternal love and wisdom are not fashionable today. Augustine, who lived in an age very similar to our own, went so far as to describe wisdom as a "foreign word." Experiencing the great emptiness of the ideologies of his time, Augustine felt a great thirst for that Truth that opens the way to Life. He understood that no one is able to reach God by his own efforts and he discovered in the end that Christ is the true Wisdom.

His work on St. Augustine was then followed by the fulfillment of yet another major undertaking that was part of the requirement for teaching at the university level, the Habilitation: He was obligated to write a book-length treatise on another theological topic. He chose to focus on another of the Church's great theologians, St. Bonaventure, a contemporary of St. Thomas Aquinas, focusing on Bonaventure's theology of history and revelation.

The process of the Habilitation was an arduous one, but he eventually won its formal acceptance in February 1957. His two studies of this period — Augustine's ecclesiology and Bonaventure's theology of history and revelation — remain two of the most significant on their subjects in the 20th century, and it can be said that he would be remembered in theological circles for these works alone, even if he had proceeded no further in his academic career.

Having earned the right to teach, Father Ratzinger received a position as a professor of theology at the Superior School of Philosophy and Theology in Freising. The academic triumphs were matched by sorrow in the young priest's life as he watched helplessly

---

Both Augustine and Bonaventure know that the Church which hopes for peace in the future is, nonetheless, obliged to love in the present; and they both realize that the kingdom of eternal peace is growing in the hearts of those who fulfill Christ's law of love in their own particular age. Both see themselves subject to the word of the Apostle: "So there remain faith, hope, and love, these three. But the greatest of these is love" (1 Cor. 13,13).

— EXCERPT FROM
THE THEOLOGY OF HISTORY IN ST. BONAVENTURE
BY JOSEPH RATZINGER (P. 163)

while his dear father's health deteriorated following a stroke. He died on August 23, 1959 surrounded by the family.

The Young Theologian

On April 15, 1959, Father Ratzinger began lectures as a full professor of fundamental theology at the University of Bonn, embarking upon a career as a theologian that soon earned him a place among the finest theological writers of the era. He proved immediately popular with his students, displaying both a keen sense of the faith and an openness to the intellectual challenges posed in studying theology. As he described years later regarding theological inquiry:

> When you are studying theology, your intention is not to learn a trade but to understand the faith, and this presupposes, as we said a while ago, using the words of Augustine, that the faith is true, that, in other words, it opens the door to a correct understanding of your own life, of the world and of men. (*Salt of the Earth*, Ignatius Press, 1997)

The truth of what he was teaching rested at the heart of his labors, and of particular note was his embrace of the Church Fathers, an approach that was already finding much support among other theologians, including Hans Urs von Balthasar, Henri de Lubac, and Jean Danielou. In effect, as he did with his doctoral dissertation, he was plowing the immensely fertile field of the Church Fathers for ways to proclaim the truths of the faith in a modern world in such dire need of the eternal truths being offered by Christ. This endeavor, called the *Ressourcement*, or the return to sources, was not in any way a rejection of the centuries of theological inquiry, most so the Scholasticism that reached its zenith with St. Thomas Aquinas and then enjoyed a re-flowering in the late 19th century in the form of Neo-Scholasticism. Rather, it was precisely a celebration of the riches offered by the Fathers of the Church to every generation. Two books by de Lubac were particularly significant in his development, *Catholicism* and *Cor-*

pus Mysticum, both of which helped to shape his own ecclesiology, or understanding of the theology of the Church.

A year before his move to Bonn, the young theologian, like the rest of the Church, had seen the passing of Pope Pius XII. The pontiff had presided over the Church during the dark years of the Second World War and had continued to lead the faith in the years that followed. Pope Pius had labored in his last years to remain active in finding new ways for the Church's teachings to be proclaimed in the changing world after the war. In his efforts, such as relaxing the Eucharistic fast, and promoting attendance at evening Masses, the pontiff anticipated the many reforms and renewal that were soon to follow with the Second Vatican Council.

In the conclave that followed, Cardinal Angelo Roncalli, Patriarch of Venice, was elected as Pope John XXIII. The new Pope, 77 at the time of his election, was a surprise as he had not been considered a very likely choice. This proved only the first of many surprises in a momentous pontificate.

Vatican Council II

On January 25, 1959, Pope John declared his desire for three main goals to be achieved: a diocesan synod, a revision of canon law, and an ecumenical council. The synod was held in January 1960 and was a foreshadowing of the greater council to come in its effort to revitalize the life of the Roman diocese. The ecumenical council, which he called the Second Vatican Council (answering suggestions that he simply reconvene the First Vatican Council, which had never adjourned), was to prove the most important event in the history of the Church since the time of the Council of Trent. Said by John to be an inspiration of the Holy Spirit, the council was the fullest expression of the Pope's vision of *aggiornamento* (renewal), a new vibrant presentation of the faith.

On May 16, 1959, Cardinal Domenico Tardini was appointed the head of the first preparatory commission with the task of consulting with the prelates of the Church throughout the globe and the esteemed theologians of the Catholic universities. On June 29, Pope John issued the encyclical *Ad Petri cathedram* in which he gave formal explanation of the purpose of the council. The next year, he wrote the *motu proprio Superno Dei nutu* (June 5, 1960), by which he announced the appointment of a preparatory commission and other ancillary and subordinate commissions and secretariats. John himself headed the central commission and appointed curial Cardinals to preside over the others with the exception of the Secretariat on Communications Media, under Archbishop Martin O'Connor, rector of the North American College.

These commissions initiated their work in November 1960 and were finished in June 1962. The previous year, on Christmas Day, John published the apostolic constitution *Humanae salutis*, instructing the council to begin in 1962. By the *motu proprio Concilium* (February 2, 1962), he placed the opening of the proceedings at October 2, 1962. After commending the assembly to the protection of St. Joseph, on July 1, 1962, he asked all Catholics to do penance in anticipation of the work of the Council Fathers through the encyclical *Paenitentiam agere*.

John had as his stated goals the renewal of the Church, its modernization to facilitate the accomplishment of its mission in the modern world, and thereby to foster the unity of all Christians. He used the term *aggiornamento* (updating) to describe the aim of his program and hopes. At the opening session (October 11), attended by 2,540 prelates, the Pope stressed the distinctly positive nature of his call.

The council was given its organization by the *motu proprio Appropinquante concilio* (August 2, 1962). There were to be three types of meetings: commissions of twenty-four members; general congregations where first votes and discussions would be held; and public sessions, headed by the Pope, at which final votes on the assorted documents would be taken.

At the first congregation of December 13, 1962, in Session I, two Cardinals, Joseph Frings of Cologne and Achille Liénart of Lille, requested that the Council Fathers should adjourn until December 16 so as to familiarize themselves with possible candidates for the commissions and be granted the right to choose their own commission members instead of the ones picked by the Curia.

After the close of the first session, the remaining deliberations would be presided over by a new pontiff. Increasingly ill, John had attended the last meeting of the session with difficulty. His health deteriorated over the early part of 1963, and he died on June 3. In the resulting conclave, the Cardinals chose Cardinal Giovanni Montini, Archbishop of Milan, on June 21, 1963, Pope Paul VI. Montini had been a clear favorite on entering the conclave and had been used extensively by John in the preparation for the council. Besides being considered the chosen successor of John, Montini also clearly desired to continue the council in the Johannine tradition. His eulogy of Pope John — declaring that the council must continue on the path chosen by John — and his own statements of approval were said by many observers to have been critical to his election.

Work resumed on September 29, 1963, and the sessions went on for two years. The result was embodied in the sixteen documents promulgated by the council, two dogmatic and two pastoral constitutions, nine decrees, and three declarations. Pope Paul solemnly closed the council on December 8, 1965.

Father Ratzinger and the Council

Speaking about the Council in an interview in 1985, then Cardinal Ratzinger observed:

> Whoever accepts Vatican II, as it has been clearly expressed and understood itself, at the same time accepts the whole binding tradition of the Catholic Church, particularly also the two previous councils. And that also applies to the so-called "progressivism," at least in its extreme forms . . . It is likewise impossible to decide in favor of Trent and Vatican I and against Vatican II. Whoever denies Vatican II denies the authority that upholds the other two councils and thereby detaches them from their foundation. (*The Ratzinger Report*, Ignatius Press, 1985)

As a young theologian, Father Joseph Ratzinger viewed the summoning of the Second Vatican Council as a major opportunity for the Church to bring authentic renewal and reform and to achieve — as Pope John had hoped — a way of proclaiming the Gospel in new ways to a world transformed by the war and the massive changes wrought by the intellectual and social upheavals of the time. At its opening session, he was only 35, but he had already proven both respected and very popular. The opinion held of him by other theologians and figures during the council was to increase considerably by its conclusion.

Crucial to Father Ratzinger's involvement in the council was the very signifcant position enjoyed by Cardinal Josef Frings of Cologne. As seen, he had an influential voice in shaping the direction of the early period of the council along with other very prominent supporters of reform such as Cardinals Suenens of Brussels, Bernard Alfrink of Utrecht, Julius Döpfner of Munich-Freising; and Franz König of Vienna. Frings was a key figure, for example, in securing a delay in the deliberations until the several thousand bishops could get to know each other better, familiarize themselves with the work to be done, and even choose their own commission members for the various committees that would be drafting the documents of the council. This move, approved by Pope John, significantly altered the atmosphere, proceedings, and direction of the commissions and the council itself. Cardinal Frings went to play a role in shaping other events over the next several years as the council fathers carried on their work in Rome.

Father Ratzinger had come to Cardinal Frings' attention early on in the period after the announcement of the new ecumenical council, chiefly through his old seminary friend, Father Herbert Luthe, by then Cardinal Frings' personal secretary. The Archbishop of Cologne met with the young priest and instantly liked him, so much so that when the council began he appointed Father Ratzinger to the position of *peritus*, meaning that he was to be one of a large group of theologians named to provide advice and assistance to the bishops taking part. As it turned out, the council was marked by the significant involvement of the *periti* in the drafting of the actual documents, and Father Ratzinger was no exception. Indeed, he was instrumental in advising Cardinal Frings and so was a direct contributor to the ultimate success of the council.

In Rome, Cardinal Frings and his staff took up residence in the Anima, the house for German-speaking priests and seminarians in Rome. Father Ratzinger proved indefatigable in his work as an advisor and was soon a widely seen figure giving lectures in Rome and in Germany on the work of the council. He was especially popular among the German-speaking seminarians who looked up to him as one of the most eloquent speakers on the need for the council and the value of its work for the Church.

More important was his work for the German-speaking bishops. Having earned the complete confidence of Cardinal Frings in the time leading up to the council, Father Ratzinger was given several key assignments, including briefing the German-speaking bishops on the drafts of the documents and then setting to work on the specific schemas of several key documents — the planned constitutions on revelation (what became *Dei Verbum*) and the Church (*Lumen Gentium*). Ratzinger was brought into close contact with another even more eminent theologian in this effort, Karl Rahner. Seminary students of the period, in fact, still remember that among the professors who were considered mandatory hearing during those fateful years were Ratzinger and Rahner.

The two priests collaborated most effectively on the decree on revelation, and both became key to the long period that followed throughout the council of committees, subcommittees, meetings, discussions, and deliberations among theologians and the bishops. In a short time, Ratzinger had become a fixture among the leading theologians of the Church and was included, for example, as a member of the key subcommission charged by the Doctrinal Committee with the immense task of developing the schema for the document that incorporated the comments and concerns of the bishops in the council. Ratzinger served with such luminaries as Rahner, Alois Grillmeier, Otto Semmelroth, and Yves Congar. To the delight and relief of the theologians who toiled on it, the Dogmatic Constitution on Divine Revelation, *Dei Verbum*, was approved on November 18, 1965, one of the last documents to be voted on by the bishops as the council drew to a close.

Father Ratzinger was also a significant participant in the drafting of the schema for *Lumen Gentium*, the central document on the Church. Named to the fifth subcommittee by the Doctrinal Commission, Father Ratzinger sat with Rahner again and two other theologians, Salaverri and Maccarrone, to deal with the topic of collegiality. In the end, he had a direct role in shaping several articles in the document, specifically in Chapter Three, articles 22 and 23 that spelled out the Church's understanding of collegiality. The Dogmatic Constitution on the Church, *Lumen Gentium*, was approved on November 21, 1964. Father Ratzinger was also invited to assist in the drafting of the decree on the Church's missionary activity. That document was approved as *Ad Gentes*, Decree on the Church's Missionary Activity, on December 7, 1965.

Even as the council was progressing in 1963, Father Ratzinger received word that his mother, like his father only four years before, was approaching the end. She died on December 16, 1963, in the same way as her beloved Joseph — surrounded by her children and having departed the world in the embrace of the Church.

The Post-Conciliar Upheaval

There is no question that Father Ratzinger had been an active and notable *peritus* throughout the Second Vatican Council. He had gone to the council eager to take part in its deliberations and to share his gifts for the renewal of the Church. And he had made some major contributions. He left with great enthusiasm and with the same general sense of optimism that surrounded the good feelings of the council fathers at the conclusion of their four year journey together in Rome. His verdict on the documents and those efforts many years later is an unequivocal one. As he said in *The Ratzinger Report* in 1985:

> Cardinal Julius Döpfner once remarked that the Church of the post-conciliar period is a huge construction site. But a critical spirit later added that it was a construction site where the blueprint had been lost and everyone continues to build according to his taste. The result is evident . . . Vatican II in its official promulgations, in its authentic documents, cannot be held responsible for this development which on the contrary, radically contradicts both the letter and the spirit of the Council Fathers.

The loss of the "blueprint" became evident very quickly after the Second Vatican Council ended in 1965. With the conclusion of the council, Father Ratzinger returned full-time to the halls of academia. In 1963, he began teaching at the University of Münster, and assumed, in 1966, a second chair in dogmatic theology at the University of Tübingen. The latter university was already well-known as a leading center in theological studies, boasting such eminent faculty members as Rahner and Hans Küng.

The mood in the wake of the council and even more so the prevailing mood of the times was of freedom on the march, openness to innovation, and liberalization. A sharp radicalization of the campuses in the late 1960s was accompanied by student protests against the Vietnam War, academic authority, and the teachings of the Catholic faith. The hopes of *aggiornamento* as a dialogue between the Church and the world, however, soon became at times a monologue delivered by modern culture, to the great detriment of the Church.

Ratzinger notes in his memoirs that he embarked upon his teaching at Tübingen in a state of considerable physical exhaustion after the council, and he was forced to commute between the towns of Münster and Tübingen. In Münster, there were whispers of revolution, but it was in Tübingen that the full shout of chaos was heard. What he calls the faculties' listening to the "signs of the times" became more radicalized and more distressing, and he remembers that the last moment of true peace at the university was the celebration in1967 of the 150th anniversary of the creation of the faculty of theology.

By 1968, Ratzinger saw his fellow professors abandoning the Catholic faith in favor of radical intellectual fads and a creeping Marxist ideology that went beyond a poor interpretation of the council to the conscious rejection of divine revelation. Chief among the most severe influences were Ernst Bloch with his Marxist analysis of the Christian faith and Jurgen Moltmann, who was responsible for crafting the "Theology of Hope" that encouraged Christian participation in social revolution.

He watched in horror as professors in the theology department who ought to have been standing firm as a bulwark against the Marxist ideology on campus became its leaders. In a mockery of authentic Catholic teaching, some professors took the notions of biblical hope in the messiah and transformed it into a radical call for what he termed "Marxist messianism" that drained God from the content of Scripture and replaced the divine with political activism. God is no longer the center of life but the political movement — the party — becomes the end all of human activity, an atheistic piety as he terms it that sacrifices the human in its pursuit of the realization of ideology. For the theologian, this means that God is supplanted by the party.

To Ratzinger's great sadness, Tübingen was soon the heart of this Marxist tendency, and Ratzinger wrote of the consequences stemming from this triumph of the radical culture of the period: "There was an instrumentalization by ideologies that were tyrannical, brutal, and cruel. That experience made it clear to me that the abuse of the faith had to be resisted if one wanted to uphold the will of the council." (*Salt of the Earth*, Ignatius Press, 1997)

In effect, he was seeing play out in the halls of Tübingen and other theological centers of learning a collapse of faith in the face of a toxic ideology that was similar to that faced by Bavaria thirty years before. The ideologies were radically different in their approaches, but the results for the Catholic faith and well-being of the human person were essentially the same.

Ratzinger was shocked as well by the response to *Humanae Vitae*, the papal encyclical by Pope Paul VI on July 29, 1968, that affirmed the Church's teaching on the use of artificial contraception. The levels of dissent by theologians all over the world, including those of Germany, only added to his alarm about the state of theology at Tübingen.

Regensburg

By the end of 1968, Father Ratzinger had endured enough. He had to depart from the university. The time had come for action. As he saw little prospect of bringing genuine change at Tübingen, however, he accepted a complete change of atmosphere and headed back to Bavaria and a starkly different situation. A new university was being established by the local Bavarian government in the city of Regensburg, and Ratzinger was asked to assist. Ratzinger had served as a member of the committee for academic appointments and had been asked to assume the chair of dogmatic theology. Initially, he refused as he was tired of moving around from school to school and had looked forward to remaining at Tübingen. Events proved contrary to his hopes, and in late 1968 he was approached again by the university with the offer of a second chair in dogma that was to be established (the first offered chair had been filled by a friend, Johann Auer). He found himself once more able to teach theology without the struggles with Marxism and camouflaged atheism.

Located on the right bank of the Danube River, Regensburg (also known as Ratisbon) is dominated by its magnificent medieval buildings, especially the patricians' houses, the *Steinerne Brücke* (Stone Bridge) across the Danube, and the Cathedral of St. Peter, arguably the most important Gothic church in the whole of Bavaria. There was thus much to entice a cultured and learned theology professor, but Regensburg offered additional inducements.

The position also permitted him to be near his brother, Georg who by now was established in his own right as a Domkapellmeister (conductor) of the chief choir in Regensburg, the famed Regensburger Domspatzen. The choir took part in 1965 at the closing of the Vatican Council, and Georg remained Kapellmeister from 1964 to 1994 and eventually retired as a Monsignor, a Protonotary Apostolic, and a holder of the Bavarian Order of Merit.

The initial time in Regensburg had a decided makeshift feel as the buildings for the campus were not yet completed. Theology, for example, was taught in part in the Theological College that had belonged to the community of the Dominicans in the city with its attached church that lent such a beautiful atmosphere to instruction. In time, as the university took shape, Ratzinger became dean and vice president, claiming among his students a number of theologians who have gone on to their own international fame, such as the Jesuit Joseph Fessio of the United States and Christoph Schönborn, who became one of the principal architects of the *Catechism of the Catholic Church*, the Archbishop of Vienna in 1995, and a Cardinal in 1998.

The same year that he began at Regensburg, he was appointed by Pope Paul VI a member of the International Theological Commission of the Holy See, a position he held from 1969 until 1980. His appointment was a kind of validation from the Holy See that his efforts to defend the truth at Tübingen were the correct course. In the course of his activities for the newly established Commission, he met and had immensely fruitful discourse with the finest of the theologians of the time, including Hans Urs von Balthasar, Henri de Lubac, Philippe Delhaye, and M.-J. Le Guillou. Von Balthasar and de Lubac especially went on to become towering figures in the struggle to recapture authentic theology from the politicized and radical interpretations then being advanced in so many quarters of the Church. Both de Lubac and von Balthasar were recognized for their toil by being named Cardinals in the years just prior to their deaths.

Inspired by the new atmosphere, Ratzinger was also embarking upon a new period of theological writing during which he firmly

JOSEPH RATZINGER
THE THEOLOGIAN

Owing to his later work and international fame as Prefect of the Congregation of the Doctrine of the Faith, the place of Joseph Ratzinger as one of the leading theologians of the modern Church has at times been forgotten. He established himself squarely in the great tradition of accomplished 20th-century theologians through his two groundbreaking studies on ecclesiology in Augustine and history and revelation in Bonaventure and then built on these with contributions to journals, periodicals, essays, and additional studies. His theological concerns have covered a vast number of topics, including ecclesiology, sacramental theology, liturgical studies, catechesis, Christology, Eschatology, and biblical theology. He played a consequential role in the drafting of the Vatican II documents *Dei Verbum* and *Lumen Gentium*. He is also the author of the renowned text, *Introduction to Christianity* and such prominent theological works as *Principles of Catholic Theology, Behold the Pierced One, Called to Communion, The Spirit of the Liturgy,* and *God is Near Us: The Eucharist the Heart of Life.* Especially revealing are *Milestones,* published in 1998, a memoir of his life until 1977, and his appointment as Archbishop of Munich and Freising and *The Ratzinger Report, Salt of the Earth,* and *God and the World: Believing and Living in Our Time* detailed interviews that cover his views on the Second Vatican Council and the problems faced by post-conciliar Church.

Central to his theology is one overriding conviction: the pursuit of objective Truth. The Truth is a thread weaving all of his labors together, both as a theologian and as a priest, a bishop, a Cardinal, and finally as Pope. It is given its most visible testament in his choice of episcopal motto: *Cooperatores Veritatis* ("Co-Workers With the Truth"; 3 Jn 8).

established himself publicly against the tides that were then rocking the ship of Catholic thought. As he declared in an interview years later, "I think that, in those years, I learned where discussion must stop, because it is turning into a lie, and resistance must start in order to maintain freedom."

In 1968, he published *Einführung in das Christentum* (*Introduction to Christianity*), a work he intended to serve as a basic introduction to the Christian faith and that went on to become a standard text in many college courses for basic theology. The work itself emerged out of a series of his lectures at Tübingen in 1967 and was structured around his meditations upon the Apostles Creed. The power of the book's structure and logic and its continuing value were explained by Msgr. Lorenzo Albacete in a column he wrote immediately after the new Pope's election:

> The book's premise was that we were living at a time in which the Christian proposal for life was no longer understood. The Christian vocabulary had become incomprehensible to many people. For this reason, the author went over all the items of the official Christian Creed, relating each one to a concrete experience of life. I realized that the doctrines of the church were not ideas to be accepted as abstract truths. Instead, each single one was linked to an experience of life that could be verified as truly corresponding to how we are made, to what it means to be human, to those needs in the heart of each human being that we all seek to fulfill, such as the need for freedom, for friendship, for beauty, for truth. Faith, the book explained, is an encounter with a 'You' that sustains us, and Who, in the midst of the definitive needs of our humanity, offers us the promise of an indestructible love that never ends. Faith sustains all our efforts to fulfill the needs of the heart and gives us hope that what we look for can be found. (*New York Daily News*, April 2005)

In 1971, he gave a public lecture at the Bavarian Catholic Academy in Munich with the title, "Why I Am Still in the Church." He asked of his audience difficult questions about the state of the Church in the wake of the council. But he expressed a theme that has been consistent throughout regarding the council: "How is it possible that in the very moment in which the council seemed to have harvested the mature crop of the awakening of the previous decades, instead of these fulfilling riches, it produced a frightening emptiness?" His answer was clear — and it was one that continues to resonate: "one can be Christian only inside the Church, not beside her."

By the early 1970's he was likewise despairing of the direction of the journal *Concilium* of which he was a founding member. The journal had been established to continue the discussions of the Second Vatican Council. It included some of the most prominent theologians of the conciliar era, including Rahner, Küng, Johannes Metz, Edward Schillebeeckx, de Lubac, and von Balthasar, as well as Joseph Ratzinger. As the years passed, the journal seemed in Ratzinger's view — and that of several friends and colleagues — to have abandoned the authentic direction of the council and to have wandered into misrepresentations of its documents and intent.

In reply, in 1972, together with von Balthasar, de Lubac and others, he launched the theological journal *Communio*, a quarterly review of Catholic theology and culture that became one of the best sources for Ratzinger's theological explorations. The journal served as well as a forum for other theologians who were disenchanted with *Concilium's* outlook, including two younger Germans, Walter Kasper and Karl Lehmann, both of whom went on to become bishops and then Cardinals in 2001.

While at Regensburg, he also embarked upon an ambitious collaborative effort with his friend and colleague Johann Auer, to create a comprehensive study of theology that eventually appeared as the nine-volume collection, *Kleine Katholische Dogmatik*. Ratzinger's primary contribution to the series was a study on eschatology, or the Four Last Things (Death and Judgment, Heaven and Hell).

The time in Regensburg was clearly one of the happiest in Ratzinger's life. He built himself a small house that became his home — complete with a garden — for himself and his sister who had been serving for years as his utterly reliable secretary and friend. Georg was able to visit frequently, and for the first time since the death of their father in 1959 and the passing of their mother in 1963, the three siblings were gathered together as a family. This happy situation was not to last as Father Ratzinger was soon to be summoned from the peaceful medieval city on the Danube to the highest precincts of the Catholic Church.

Chapter 8

CO-WORKERS WITH
THE TRUTH

——————✠——————

Cooperatores Veritatis (Co-Workers With the Truth)

— EPISCOPAL MOTTO OF JOSEPH CARDINAL RATZINGER

A New Archbishop for Munich and Freising

Father Ratzinger's theological writings, his teaching, and his lectures did not exist in a vacuum. His departure from Tübingen's hostile atmosphere and his defense of both the authentic teachings of the Second Vatican Council and the Magisterium had earned him recognition in many ecclesiastical circles, including those of Rome. During the council, Ratzinger and other prominent *periti*, or theological consultants, had won considerable fame for their efforts, and one of the most grateful of the leaders at the council had been the one-time Cardinal Giovanni Battista Montini who was elected in 1963 as Pope Paul VI. At the end of the Council, Pope Paul VI had predicted great things for both Hans Küng and Joseph Ratzinger. Papal recognition was not long delayed with Father Ratzinger's appointment to the International Theological Commission in 1969.

On July 24, 1976, the whole of Bavaria was stunned to learn of the sudden death of Cardinal Julius Döpfner, the Archbishop of Munich and Freising, whom Ratzinger had known well since the Second Vatican Council. The see of Munich and Freising was now vacant, and rumors and speculation began to swirl as to who might be named as the new Archbishop. To his genuine surprise, Ratzinger started hearing quiet word that his name was being discussed as a pos-

145

sible successor. He dismissed these claims as idle gossip, but a little concern may have entered his mind when he received a request from the apostolic nuncio for Germany, Archbishop Guido del Mestri, for a brief visit on some pretext. The nuncio, or papal representative, sat down with the theology professor in Regensburg and chatted briefly. He then handed Ratzinger a letter, asking him to read it, think it over, and inform him of his decision. The letter declared that Pope Paul VI had appointed him the Archbishop of Munich and Freising.

Ratzinger requested permission to ponder, pray, and reflect on the important office he was being offered, and he specifically requested permission to speak with his confessor, who happened to be his friend, Johann Auer. When, however, Ratzinger asked his friend's advice, Father Auer was adamant in advising him to accept. Returning to the nuncio in the hotel at which the papal representative was staying for the visit, Ratzinger took a sheet of hotel stationery and wrote a formal letter of acceptance.

The announcement of his appointment as Archbishop of Munich and Freising was made on March 24, 1977. The appointment was remarkable in that Father Ratzinger was a trained theologian with virtually no experience in a chancery office, one of the traditional training grounds for bishops. Likewise, he was barely fifty years old, making him quite young to assume so significant an archdiocese in Germany.

On May 28, 1977, Joseph Aloysius Ratzinger was consecrated Archbishop of Munich and Freising. He remembers that the day of the consecration was a bright and beautiful one in the city, but in his own mind and heart he greeted the event with some trepidation owing to the burdens he was about to receive. The ceremony itself, though, filled him with such joy and the sacramental reality that he was buoyed and inspired for the work of the episcopacy that was to come.

Joseph Ratzinger had gone from a respected theologian seen as a counter-revolutionary of sorts in the struggle for the soul of theological studies to the archbishop of one of the key sees in Germany, an archdiocese dating back to the 8th century. He was suddenly the shepherd over the Catholic Church in his own beloved Bavaria with responsibility for the spiritual well-being of the people he had known since his birth. Pope Paul VI had given him the firmest approbation of his efforts for the faith possible, but the pontiff wasted no time in adding further to his obvious esteem for the new archbishop. Only a few days after the consecration, the Pope made the public announcement that he had named five new Cardinals, One of the new Cardinals was Archbishop Ratzinger.

On June 27, 1977, Pope Paul elevated Archbishop Ratzinger to the rank of Cardinal. The new Cardinal-designate traveled to Rome to receive the red biretta, the traditional symbol of elevation to the Sacred College of Cardinals, from the hand of the Pope. Designated a Cardinal priest, he was granted as his titular church that of Santa Maria Consolatrice al Tiburtino. The Consistory was slightly different from normal ones in that only five new Cardinals were being installed to the Sacred College, including an *in pectore* Cardinal who had been unaware of his nomination. With Cardinal Ratzinger were named Giovanni Benelli, Archbishop of Florence; Bernardin Gantin, from Benin, who was then serving in the Roman Curia; Luigi Ciappi, a Dominican and papal theologian; and Frantisek Tomasek of Prague, who had actually been named a Cardinal in 1976 but in secret, or *in pectore*, meaning that Pope Paul would not reveal the name at the time owing to the fact that the Cardinal-elect lived in a country where his appointment might have damaged Church-State relations with the Communist dictatorship. By 1977, Pope Paul felt that the circumstances permitted the appointment being made public.

As he remembered years later in an interview in 2003 with the Italian magazine *30 Giorni*, Cardinal Ratzinger became the inadvertent focus of attention in the consistory because of the fact that the other Cardinals lacked their own entourages. The Consistory was an unusually small one — normally more Cardinals are named — and the other four each brought with them only small groups of friends and family. Cardinal Benelli had only recently been named to Florence, Cardinal Gantin's friends had trouble traveling from Benin, Cardinal Ciappi was known by very few outside of Rome, and Cardinal Tomasek's friends struggled to receive permission to leave Czechoslovakia. So, Cardinal Ratzinger's large and excited group of supporters sounded even more boisterous in the Paul VI Hall in the Vatican. Pope Paul, Cardinal Ratzinger realized, was quite pleased with the enthusiasm of the Catholics from Munich and Freising as it seemed to confirm that he had the made the right choice in their new archbishop.

The new Cardinal was then invited to have a private audience with the Pope and admitted that his natural shyness and unfamiliarity with the highest reaches of the Church left him uncertain in his actions. The Pope reassured him, and the two had a pleasant conversation. He met Pope Paul again during his *ad limina* visit son after and then again in the fall for his 80th birthday.

Cardinal Ratzinger settled into his duties in Munich with a quiet and steady determination to be a true pastor to his people. This objective was given little time to become reality considering the surprising events that took place barely a year after his installation as archbishop. While on holiday in Austria, he received a call on August 6, 1978, from the Vicar General of Munich and Freising that the Pope was gravely ill. He soon had another call that the Pope had died. Pope Paul VI had passed away at the age of 81 at Castel Gandolfo after a reign of fifteen years. The passing of the Pope signaled the start of a *sede vacante* that required Cardinal Ratzinger to travel to Rome and take part in the papal funeral and the conclave.

During the weeks that followed Pope Paul's passing, Cardinal Ratzinger was given the opportunity to meet and get to know the other members of the College. Some he had known for many years, such as Bernard Alfrink of Utrecht, Joseph Höffner of Cologne, Franz König of Austria, and Leo Suenens of Mechelen-Brussels. The conclave, however, was also a gathering of an entirely new generation of Cardinals who had been appointed in the years after the council. Ratzinger was one of the better known — albeit most recently named

THE MOOR, THE SCALLOP SHELL, AND THE BEAR

At the time of his appointment as Archbishop of Munich and Freising, Archbishop-elect Ratzinger was obligated by custom to adopt a coat-of-arms that would serve as a kind of visual statement as to his own priorities and sensibilities as a bishop. Cardinal Ratzinger concluded his memoirs, *Milestones*, with a meditation on its design, giving an explanation for each of the elements. There are three key symbols, a Moor wearing a crown, a scallop shell, and a bear with a pack on its back. The first element, the Moor, was required for his coat-of-arms as it had been the symbol of the Archbishops of Munich and Freising for a millennium. Called the "Moor of Freising," the image has defied explanation, and no one is entirely certain how the tradition began. Cardinal Ratzinger suggested in his reflection that it depicted the Church's universality and the truth that "you are all one in Christ Jesus" (Gal. 3:28).

The scallop shell, the first of two personal additions, has long been used as the emblem of pilgrims, such as those who journeyed to Santiago de Compostela, and was intended to suggest that "here we have no lasting city" (Heb. 13:14). The shell also evokes the teaching of St. Augustine who used it to express the mystery of the Holy Trinity. The great saint once discovered a child on the beach trying to fill a hole in the sand with water from the sea by scooping in water with the scallop shell. For Augustine, such a fruitless effort mirrored his own labors to comprehend the vast mystery of God.

The bear with a backpack was a symbol from the legend of Freising's patron, St. Corbinian. While traveling to Rome, Corbinian met a bear that attacked the horse which was carrying the saint's baggage. To punish the bear, Corbinian forced it to carry his pack all the way to Rome. For Ratzinger the bear suggested the weight of episcopal authority and also

Augustine's meditation on Psalm 73 and his lesson on the tests of faith. Remarkably, Psalm 73 was in prayed in the Office of Readings (the official prayer of the Church) on the first day of the conclave.

These symbols were retained when Cardinal Ratzinger became Pope Benedict XVI and approved his new coat-of-arms. Pope Benedict, however, introduced several other innovations into the design. He dropped the triple-tiered tiara that has traditionally appeared at the top of each Pope's coat of arms and replaced it with the miter, one of the key symbols of the bishop. The Pope also added the pallium, the woolen stole with six black crosses, representing episcopal authority, as a major element surrounding the shield, joining the ancient symbol of the crossed keys of the papacy.

The new design was created with Pope Benedict's approval by Italian Archbishop Andrea Cordero Lanza di Montezemolo, a nuncio and expert on ecclesiastical heraldry. According to the archbishop, the miter has three gold stripes to mirror the symbolism of the papal tiara's three tiers for order, jurisdiction, and magisterium. A vertical gold band connects the three stripes in the middle to demonstrate that they are united in the same person. The pallium indicates the bishop's role as pastor of the flock entrusted to him by Christ.

— members, along with Benelli, Sebastiano Baggio, Prefect of the Congregation for Bishops in Rome, and the Benedictine Basil Hume of Westminster. All three were considered *papabili* heading into the conclave, especially Benelli; Ratzinger was considered by a few to be a possibility, but his supposed candidacy, like that of Cardinal Hume, was not taken seriously as the consensus was that an Italian was likely to win. As it turned out, there was a mild surprise when Cardinal Albino Luciani, Patriarch of Venice, won election after a brief conclave on September 26 and took the name John Paul I.

Cardinal Ratzinger recalled in 2003 that he had taken an active part in the discussions leading up to the conclave among the German-speaking Cardinals, including Joseph Schröffer, then Prefect of Catholic Education, Joseph Höffner of Cologne, Franz König of Vienna, Alfred Bengsch of Berlin, and two Brazilian Cardinals, Paulo Evaristo Arns and Aloísio Lorscheider, who were of German origin. Nothing formal was decided, but the gatherings gave him the chance to spend time with his fellow Germans and German-speakers. It was clear from the conversations that Albino Luciani was the consensus of the College. He had actually met Cardinal Luciani a little over a year before when the Patriarch had come to pay a courtesy call on him while the new shepherd of Munich and Freising was on vacation and staying in the diocesan seminary of Bressanone, in the Alto-Adige.

With the new Pope installed, Cardinal Ratzinger returned to Munich and prepared to continue with his episcopal ministry. He also completed plans to travel to Ecuador to take part in a national Marian Congress to be held in Guayaquil in September. His presence in Ecuador had a special meaning as his archdiocese was twinned with the dioceses of Ecuador, and the bishops there had petitioned John Paul I to name Cardinal Ratzinger the papal delegate to the Congress.

Cardinal Ratzinger thus found himself in Quito, Ecuador, in late September as a guest of the local bishop. He had gone to bed and was sound asleep when suddenly the room was filled with bright light. The lights had been turned on, and a priest dressed in the habit of a Carmelite strode in and announced to the bewildered Cardinal that he was Alberto Lunar Tobar, then auxiliary bishop of Quito, and that it was his sad duty to inform him that the Pope was dead.

The stupefied Cardinals made their way back to Rome to choose another Pope — the man they chose would be the third Pope to reign in the year 1978. In one of the biggest surprises in Church history, the Cardinals chose as Pope the first non-Italian pontiff in 455 years and the first Polish Pope, Karol Wojtyla, Archbishop of Cracow, who took the name John Paul II.

Cardinal Ratzinger had been aware of Karol Wojtyla for some time, but the two had never had the opportunity to meet. They had exchanged copies of their books, but their worlds, despite the geographic proximity, were separated from each other by the divide of the Berlin Wall and the brooding barriers of the Soviet Empire. As George Weigel documented in his monumental biography of John Paul II, *Witness to Hope*, the two finally met during the first conclave in 1978. They shared widespread agreement on the challenges of the time and especially the crisis in the Church, in particular the need to recapture the joy and the authenticity of the Second Vatican Council. As Weigel documents, they both understood the necessity to restate for the modern world that the key to the Gospels was Truth.

Pope John Paul II set out on his unprecedented pontificate, and Ratzinger, who was rumored to have supported a Wojtylan candidacy by the time of the second conclave, went back to Munich immensely pleased with the new choice for Vicar of Christ. The next two years witnessed the whirlwind travels of the Pope across the globe, including trips to the Dominican Republic and Mexico, Poland, Ireland, and the United States, Turkey, Africa, France, and Brazil. He ended 1980 with one final trip in November, to West Germany. On the papal itinerary were visits to Bonn, Cologne, Mainz, and Munich. Cardinal Ratzinger accompanied the pontiff on his journey throughout Germany and then hosted him for the stay in Munich where the papal trip ended.

Pope John Paul was already aware of the immense gifts possessed by the Cardinal Archbishop of Munich and Freising as well as his reputation as a theologian. The close rapport that developed in these early years of the papacy, however, assumed a greater significance as the new Pope continued forward with his process of bringing genuine reform to the Roman Curia — the central government of the Church — and was seeking actively fresh minds to fill key posts in the different congregations and departments of the Holy See.

Soon after his election, the new pontiff met with Cardinal Ratzinger and offered him the position of Prefect of the Congregation for Catholic Education. Its head, the French Cardinal Gabriel-Marie Garrone, was nearing 80 and was retiring. Ratzinger was flattered and honored to be asked, but he declined on the basis that he had been Archbishop of Munich for such a short period of time.

The next year, the Yugoslavian Cardinal Franjo Seper, Prefect of the Congregation of the Doctrine of the Faith since 1968, suffered a decline in health and stepped down from his post. He died in December of that year. Once more, Pope John Paul informed Cardinal Ratzinger of his desire to bring him to Rome, this time as the head of one of the Church's most important departments, charged with insuring the purity of the Catholic faith. Cardinal Ratzinger did not refuse his pontiff. On November 25, 1981, Pope John Paul II named him Prefect of the Congregation for the Doctrine of the Faith, President of the Pontifical Biblical Commission and President of the International Theological Commission (of which he had long been a member).

Still, he took the post with not a little reluctance. As he confided to Peter Seewald in his interview published in *Salt of the Earth: Christianity and the Catholic Church at the End of the Millennium*:

> For me, the cost [of becoming Prefect of the Congregation for the Faith] was that I couldn't do full time what I had envisaged for myself, namely really contributing my thinking and speaking to the great intellectual conversation of our time, by developing an opus of my own. I had to descend to the little and various things pertaining to factual conflicts and events. I had to leave aside a great part of what would interest me and simply serve and to accept that as my task. And I had to free myself from the idea that I absolutely have to write or read this or that, I had to acknowledge that my task is here.

"My Most Uncomfortable Post"

In a famous interview aired on EWTN and conducted by host Raymond Arroyo in 2003, Cardinal Ratzinger was asked to respond

THE CONGREGATION FOR THE DOCTRINE OF THE FAITH

One of the most misunderstood departments of the Roman Curia, the Congregation for the Doctrine of the Faith is the oldest of the Curia's nine key departments (or congregations) and has as its chief purpose to safeguard the doctrine of faith and morals. Thus, it examines questions relating to Catholic doctrine and promotes the study of theology. It also evaluates theological opinions and theological writings and, when necessary and after prior consultation with concerned bishops, admonishes those who have exceeded the principles of the faith. Reproving writers takes place only after the authors have been given the opportunity to defend themselves in a process of examination that normally takes years and involves numerous sessions of discussion and review. While the Congregation is perceived as engaging in merely negative activities of evaluation and the condemnation of error, it is also very active in positive efforts on behalf of the faith and in the promotion of orthodox doctrine.

The Congregation was founded officially in 1542 by Pope Paul III under the title of the Sacred Congregation of the Universal Inquisition, and its chief duty was to defend the Church from heresy. Pope St. Pius X in 1908 changed the name to the Sacred Congregation of the Holy Office. This was again changed in 1965 by Pope Paul VI to its present designation.

The rules by which the Congregation operates today were published in Article 48 of the Apostolic Constitution on the Roman Curia, *Pastor Bonus*, by John Paul II on June 28, 1988. It stipulates: "the duty proper to the Congregation for the Doctrine of the Faith is to promote and safeguard the doctrine of the faith and morals throughout the Catholic world: for this reason everything which in any way touches upon such matters falls within its competence."

to a quote from a then recent book, *God and the World*, in which he was reported to have said of his position as head of the Congregation of the Doctrine of Faith, "This is my most uncomfortable post." After laughing lightly, Cardinal Ratzinger said:

> Yes, in many senses it's uncomfortable. We have essentially and often to do with all the problems of the Church — problems of relativism, of heresies, of unacceptable theologies, difficult theologians and so on. Also with the disciplinary cases, also problem of pedophiles is our problem. We are really in this Congregation confronted with the most difficult aspects of the life of the Church today.

For over twenty-four years, Cardinal Ratzinger held one of the most challenging and demanding positions anywhere in the Church — in his hands and those of his assistants was the mandate from the Holy Father to preserve the faith, ensure doctrinal purity, and strive to keep the faithful free of scandal and confusion. The task is by its nature a very difficult one, requiring both patience and determination. In the brilliant fulfillment of his duties, Cardinal Ratzinger became the object of controversy, of scorn, of malicious misrepresentations, and also of caricature. He was given nicknames such as "God's Rottweiler," the "Panzerkardinal," "Inquisitor," and "Enforcer." He was branded a conservative extremist, a tyrant, and a hated enemy of progress in the Church.

In November 2002, Cardinal Ratzinger gave an interview to journalists during a visit to St. Anthony's Catholic University of Murcia, Spain, where he attended an International Congress on Christology. Asked about his work in the Congregation, his reply was a revealing one in terms of his own activities and that of the CDF's members:

> It is difficult to answer this in two words. We have two principal sections: one disciplinary and the other doctrinal. The disciplinary must be concerned with problems of offenses of priests, which unfortunately exist in the Church. Now we

have the great problem of pedophilia, as you know. In this case, above all, we must help the bishops to find the adequate procedures. And we are a sort of court of appeals: If someone feels unjustly treated by the bishop, he can appeal to us. The other, better known section, is the doctrinal. In this connection, Paul VI defined our task as "promoter" and "defender" of the faith. To promote, that is, to help dialogue in the family of the theologians of the world, to follow this dialogue, and encourage the positive currents, as well as to help the less positive tendencies to be conformed to the more positive ones.

The other dimension is to defend: In the context of today's world, with its relativism, with a profound opposition to the faith of the Church in many parts of the world, with agnostic, atheist, etc., ideologies, the loss of the identity of the faith takes place easily. We must help to distinguish authentic novelties, authentic progress, from other steps that imply a loss of the identity of the faith . . .

For us, cooperation with the bishops is fundamental. If possible, the bishops must resolve the problems. However, it is often theologians of international renown and, therefore, the problem goes beyond the possibilities of a bishop. So it is taken to the congregation. Here, we promote the dialogue with these theologians to arrive, if possible, to a peaceful solution. Only in very few cases is there a negative solution.

Lost in the caricatures and the accusations were several notable aspects to his long and faithful service to the Pope. First, there was the simple fact that he acted throughout his 24 years with the complete trust and confidence of John Paul II and that he was doing the task he was asked to undertake. As such, it is impossible to separate his work at the Congregation for the Doctrine of the Faith (CDF) from the wider aspirations, program, and vision of the pontificate of John Paul II.

George Weigel suggested in his study of John Paul II that Ratzinger fit superbly into the overall vision for the Church of the Pope. He was the perfect choice by the Pope for a genuine renewal of theology as he arrived with his own decades of experience as a respected theological expert rather than an old veteran who would run the CDF as merely a department. He was also a significant departure in his own background in Augustine and Bonaventure and the *Ressourcement* from the traditional Scholastic training of previous prefects; in this, Weigel saw Ratzinger as a demonstration of theological pluralism at work without the sacrifice of orthodoxy. As Weigel writes in *Witness to Hope* (HarperCollins, 1998), "Wojtyla recognized in the shy, scholarly Ratzinger a contemporary intellectual who was a more accomplished theologian than himself. Together they made a formidable intellectual team."

The two were the closest of collaborators, consulting frequently on all matters of importance facing the Church and authentic Church teachings. They met in private every Friday night — when the Pope was in Rome or when his health permitted in the last years — to discuss the business of the CDF and had cordial and lively luncheons on Tuesdays at which a wide-ranging series of topics might be discussed and shared with other participants. Throughout the long years, as Cardinal Ratzinger was savaged by critics and accused of extremism, the pontiff remained firmly with him and gave him his support. Toward the end of his life, Pope John Paul called him, "my trusted friend."

By the 1990s, according to Cardinal Ratzinger's own statements, he was ready to retire, but in a conversation he had with the Pope, John Paul said to him, "We're both getting old, Joseph. We must continue to work together." As Cardinal Ratzinger related in his EWTN interview, he had wanted to step down in 1991, 1996, and 2001, with the hope of returning to his writing and study, in much the same way as had Cardinal Carlo Martini, the former Archbishop of Milan and a noted biblical scholar. What compelled him to remain at work in the vineyard was the example of the Holy Father. As he put it in the interview:

> But on the other hand, seeing the suffering Pope, I cannot say to the Pope, "I will retire. I will write my books" . . . Seeing him, how he is giving himself, I have to continue . . . His suffering is in communion with the suffering of Christ, and perhaps with his suffering we can better understand that the suffering of Christ has redeemed the world — in giving himself in suffering, giving up something, giving up some activities sometime but that really himself is the presence of the force of the deeper dimensions of human beings. We can learn from him that suffering and the gift of himself is an essential gift we need in our time.

As Prefect of the CDF, Cardinal Ratzinger was fulfilling the task he saw needed to be done for the good of the Church. The mandate of the Congregation — as stipulated by the papal reforms of the Curia in the 1988 apostolic constitution *Pastor Bonus* — was to provide a corrective for errors among the faithful in the pursuit of doctrinal purity and to advise the members of the Church in matters of pressing importance in faith and morals. For this, no apology was needed, even if the issues he confronted proved controversial.

The demands of his position as head of the CDF entailed Cardinal Ratzinger's direct involvement in virtually every major doctrinal issue of the long pontificate of John Paul II. Three examples serve to illustrate the nature of his work: Liberation Theology; the relationship between the Church and the world's other religions; and celebrated cases involving individual theologians whose writings were examined by the CDF and found to be in error.

Liberation Theology

By the time of his appointment as Prefect of the CDF, Cardinal Ratzinger was well aware of the proliferation of the multi-faceted movement that brought several theologies together under the collective title of "Liberation Theology" that had come into prominence in the years after the Second Vatican Council.

The Church has always offered the unfailing teaching that the Gospel of Jesus Christ is a message of freedom and liberation, specifically liberation from the radical slavery of sin. As such, its aim and its end is to bring freedom through the gift of grace and liberation from the many different kinds of slavery found in human existence, including those forms of slavery in the cultural, economic, social, and political spheres that all derive ultimately from sin and that establish obstacles to living in the truth and deprive women and men of their authentic dignity. The term "liberation" is thus a fundamental one in the Old and New Testaments, and there is legitimacy in the examination of a "theology of liberation" that reflects on the biblical theme of liberation and freedom, on its practical realization, and on the call for an authentic evangelical spirit that embodies a "preferential option for the poor."

Such an option has found rich expression in recent papal writings, in particular the social encyclicals of Pope John Paul II such as *Laborem Exercens* (On Human Work), *Sollicitudo Rei Socialis* (On Social Concerns), and *Centesimus Annus* (The Hundredth Year; referring to the great encyclical of Pope Leo XIII, *Rerum Novarum*, "On New Things," that launched modern Catholic social teachings). Liberation is, consequently, a common theme in modern times, but it is one rooted firmly in the authentic teachings of the Church in light of the specific message of revelation and interpreted by the Magisterium of the Church.

In the years after the Council, however, there were currents of thought regarding liberation that assumed not liberation from sin and its dehumanizing manifestations in the world but liberation that advocated political, economic, and social revolution, often along clearly Marxist lines. Such a collective set of liberation theologies was first seen at work in Latin America as early as the 1950s and 1960s out of a desire to change the prevailing social structures of the period in Central and South America where poverty was endemic, where dictatorships oppressed their citizens, and where Western exploitative capitalism was considered in some quarters as the chief cause of problems in the hemisphere. From the start, theologies of liberation were difficult to define, for such an expression could be understood entirely within the context of the Church's special concern for the poor and the victims of oppression, and a resulting commitment to justice.

As they developed, there were several contradictory theological positions being advanced as "Liberation Theology" in Latin America and then elsewhere around the world. The precise doctrinal boundaries were not defined well and their own ambiguities of language left them open to manipulation and misunderstanding. The great risk that attended these approaches was their apparent emphasis on liberation from slavery and oppression in exclusively earthly or temporal forms. Liberation from sin is demoted to a place of secondary importance. In its most extreme form, the language of liberation theology carried overtones of Marxism and the Marxist revolutionary ideas being promoted throughout Central America by guerrilla movements. For those uneducated in the nuances at work, the language of liberation gave them the sense of freedom to become involved actively in the Marxist movements of Nicaragua and El Salvador, and even to support the dictatorship of Fidel Castro and the Soviet Union's exporting of revolutionary Communism into the Third World. Turmoil resulted, then, over the ambiguities, the misinterpretations, and the uncertainties as to what exactly Liberation Theology actually meant. Pope John Paul II described this situation succinctly in 1979 when he visited Puebla, Mexico, for the gathering of Latin American Bishops. When asked what he thought of the movement, the Pope replied, "Liberation theology, yes. But *which* liberation theology?"

By the early 1980s the situation had become so tumultuous that action was deemed desirable by the Holy See. Cardinal Ratzinger and the CDF subsequently issued two instructions on the subject of liberation theology. Both instructions were criticized in the media as placing a chill on theological discourse, but both ultimately made positive contributions to the dialogue by restating the authentic teachings of the Church.

The first document was in 1984, *Libertatis Nuntius* ("Instruction on Certain Aspects of the Theology of Liberation"), and the second was in 1986, *Libertatis Conscientia* ("Instruction on Christian Freedom and Liberation"). *Libertatis Nuntius* began by recognizing the many positive contributions of the theological reflections on the Gospel's call for liberation. It spoke of the value and validity of the term "theology of liberation" and reiterated unequivocally that there was no intention to deter or discourage efforts to bring about true justice, but the "yearning for justice and for the effective recognition of the dignity of every human being needs, like every deep aspiration, to be clarified and guided." The document was concerned especially about the application of Marxist analysis to the theological question of liberation with the result that "the different theologies of liberation are situated between the 'preferential option for the poor,' . . . on the one hand, and the temptation to reduce the Gospel to an earthly gospel on the other."

Libertatis Conscientia was published as a companion document, and it was intended to be read in the context of *Libertatis Nuntius*. It addressed the issues of freedom and conscience in light of the modern experience of oppression and the call for liberation as a universal phenomenon. *Libertatis Conscientia*, however, once more situates liberation in the truth, meaning in Christ, and calls on all of the faithful to share in the proclamation of authentic liberation and freedom:

> Pastors and all those who, as priests, laity, or men and women religious, often work under very difficult conditions for evangelization and integral human advancement, should be filled with hope when they think of the amazing resources of holiness contained in the living faith of the people of God. These riches of the *sensus fidei* must be given the chance to come to full flowering and bear abundant fruit. To help the

faith of the poor to express itself clearly and to be translated into life, through a profound meditation on the plan of salvation as it unfolds itself in the Virgin of the *Magnificat* — this is a noble ecclesial task which awaits the theologian. Thus a theology of freedom and liberation which faithfully echoes Mary's *Magnificat* preserved in the Church's memory is something needed by the times in which we are living. But it would be criminal to take the energies of popular piety and misdirect them toward a purely earthly plan of liberation, which would very soon be revealed as nothing more than an illusion and a cause of new forms of slavery. Those who in this way surrender to the ideologies of the world and to the alleged necessity of violence are no longer being faithful to hope, to hope's boldness and courage, as they are extolled in the hymn to the God of mercy which the Virgin teaches us.

In the years after the promulgation of the two documents, there followed the collapse of the Soviet Union and the discrediting of Marxist theory throughout the world as a failed ideology. The practitioners of the various liberation theologies entered into a dialogue with Vatican officials and found much in common with the authentic vision of Pope John Paul II in his own teachings on liberation and freedom. Some elements of Liberation Theology went on to engage in active reformist efforts and the promotion of Catholic efforts at justice and peace in the poorest countries of the world. The promotion of the Gospel and giving voice to the poor, the defenseless, and the oppressed remains a priority for all engaged in active ministry in Africa, Latin America, and Asia where issues of globalization, AIDS, political instability, and shocking poverty remain daily crises. Other supporters went on to embrace new forms of Liberation Theology in the areas of feminism, homosexuality, and the environment. It is anticipated that new variations on the theology of liberation will arise in the 21st century, but the two documents of the CDF will remain essential foundations for judging them in light of the Gospel.

Dominus Iesus

Much as the documents on authentic liberation and freedom with regard to Liberation Theology were misrepresented in the 1980s, so too was a second equally famous statement issued by the CDF under Cardinal Ratzinger, the "Declaration on the Unicity and Salvific Universality of Jesus Christ and the Church," known by its Latin title as *Dominus Iesus*. Promulgated on August 6, 2000, with the statement at its end that it had been done so with "the sure knowledge and by his apostolic authority, ratified and confirmed" by Pope John Paul II, the declaration was attacked immediately as a blow to interreligious dialogue, and a form of fundamentalism, Roman centralism, absolutism, and a demonstration of Cardinal Ratzinger's extemism.

The criticism covered various topics, but objections chiefly centered on the claim that it allegedly took a negative view of other religious bodies, both Christian and non-Christian. The media frenzy surrounding the release of the document was accompanied by the apparent failure on the part of many of its critics to read the document itself and to rely on press statements that at times contained inaccurate accounts as to its content. One of the most singular errors in early reporting was that it claimed salvation only for Catholics. As stated in *Dominus Iesus* itself, the purpose of the document was a straightforward one:

> In the practice of dialogue between the Christian faith and other religious traditions, as well as in seeking to understand its theoretical basis more deeply, new questions arise that need to be addressed through pursuing new paths of research, advancing proposals, and suggesting ways of acting that call for attentive discernment. In this task, the present Declaration seeks to recall to Bishops, theologians, and all the Catholic faithful, certain indispensable elements of Christian doctrine, which may help theological reflection in developing solutions consistent with the contents of the faith and responsive to the pressing needs of contemporary culture. The expository language of the

Declaration corresponds to its purpose, which is not to treat in a systematic manner the question of the unicity and salvific universality of the mystery of Jesus Christ and the Church, nor to propose solutions to questions that are matters of free theological debate, but rather to set forth again the doctrine of the Catholic faith in these areas, pointing out some fundamental questions that remain open to further development, and refuting specific positions that are erroneous or ambiguous. For this reason, the Declaration takes up what has been taught in previous Magisterial documents, in order to reiterate certain truths that are part of the Church's faith.

Dominus Iesus proceeded to note that in the modern world, the "Church's constant missionary proclamation is endangered today by relativistic theories which seek to justify religious pluralism, not only *de facto* but also *de iure* (or in principle)." In answer to those dangers, the document sought to restate the teachings of the Church, drawing heavily on Scripture and, as it noted, magisterial documents. While its tone was not the "arrogant" one cited by some critics, it did adopt a nuanced and technical language as it progressed through a systematic examination of Church teachings regarding such issues as: "The Fullness and Definitiveness of the Revelation of Jesus Christ"; "The Incarnate Logos and the Holy Spirit in the Work of Salvation"; "Unicity and Universality of the Salvific Mystery of Jesus Christ"; "Unicity and Unity of the Church"; "The Church: Kingdom of God and Kingdom of Christ"; and "The Church and the Other Religions in Relation to Salvation."

Striking in its broad-ranging use of magisterial documents — in particular its fidelity to the Dogmatic Constitution on the Church, *Lumen Gentium*, of the Second Vatican Council — *Dominus Iesus* succeeded in its stated intent. As Russell Shaw wrote in an article in the 2001 edition of the *Catholic Almanac*:

> While extending encouragement to theologians seeking deeper understanding of these matters, the declaration rejects

the idea that the Church is only one way of salvation alongside others. Other religious traditions contain elements that come from God, and some of their prayers and rituals can be "preparation for the Gospel." But they lack the "salvific efficacy" of Christian sacraments; and other rituals, based on superstition or errors, are obstacles to salvation. Belief that the Church "is the instrument for the salvation of all humanity" does not lessen respect for other world religions, but it rules out the notion that "one religion is as good as another," the declaration says.

The vigorous defense of *Dominus Iesus* came from a number of quarters in the Church. Cardinal William Keeler, Archbishop of Baltimore and a leader in the Church's outreach to Judaism, said of the controversy, "The Church's teachings about our faith in the unique and redemptive role of Jesus Christ and of the Church's specific role in continuing Christ's saving mission were affirmed, as a corrective, it seems, for some misunderstandings, principally in Asia. The message of the recent document and the words of the Holy Father are not in conflict. Catholics must be true to their faith, distinct from other churches and religions." *La Civilta Cattolica*, the Jesuit magazine in Rome shared in Cardinal Keeler's comments by reminding its readers that Christianity "is not only 'a' true religion among others but is 'the' true religion and, therefore, the only religion God willed and wills for all men and women."

A crucial word on the controversy was delivered on October 1, 2000 by John Paul II himself. Addressing the faithful at the end of a Mass where he canonized 123 new saints, the Pope stated that *Dominus Iesus* was not prompted by "arrogance" but "the joyful recognition that Christ showed himself to us without any merit on our part." The Holy Father said fully:

> Our confession of Christ as the only Son, through whom we ourselves see the face of the Father, is not arrogance that shows contempt for other religions, but the joyful recognition that Christ showed himself to us without any merit on our part.

And, at the same time, he has urged us to continue to give that which we have received and also to communicate to others that which was given to us, because the Truth that was given and the Love that God is belong to all men.

The Pope also reiterate that *Dominus Iesus* did no more than follow the Second Vatican Council while adding, "It is my hope that, after so many mistaken interpretations, this heartfelt declaration will finally be able to achieve its clarifying function, as well as that of openness."

Cardinal Ratzinger restated Holy Father's defense of the document in his 2002 interview in Spain. He said,

> I am convinced that we [in *Dominus Iesus*] have interpreted Vatican II's *Lumen Gentium* in a totally faithful manner, while in the last 30 years we have increasingly attenuated the text. In fact, our critics have said to us that we have remained faithful to the letter of the Council, but we have not understood the Council. At least they acknowledge that we are faithful to the letter. The Church of Christ is not an ecumenical utopia; it is not something we make; it would not be the Church of Christ. This is why we are convinced that the Church is a Body, it is not just an idea, but this does not exclude different ways of a certain presence of the Church, even outside the Catholic Church, which are specified by the Council. I think it is evident that they exist, in so many hues, and it is understandable that this generates debates within the Church.

The Theologian and the Magisterium

Beyond the host of documents, statements, declarations, and letters issued by the CDF over his twenty-four years, Cardinal Ratzinger had as well the responsibility to evaluate theological opinions and theological writings for their doctrinal purity. Over the years, this proved another controversial undertaking owing to the various theologians whose writing and activities were examined according to the requirements laid out by the apostolic constitution *Pastor Bonus* and the long-standing purpose of the Congregation. The list was inevitably a lengthy one and included Leonardo Boff, Edward Schillebeeckx, Jacques Dupuis, Tissa Balasuriya, and Roger Haight.

A key to understanding the reason for this process of examination and why it is essential for the Church was published by the Congregation under Cardinal Ratzinger in 1990 with the full approval of Pope John Paul II in an instruction that received surprisingly little attention save in the way that it was attacked by critics as stifling academic freedom. The title of the Instruction was "On the Ecclesial Function of the Theologian" and it had as its stated purpose, "to shed light on the mission of theology in the Church."

When applied to each of the controversial decisions of the CDF over the years regarding individual theologians, the Instruction serves as both an explanation of method and a validation for action on the part of the Holy See. The Instruction also points to the obligation of Cardinal Ratzinger and the officials of the CDF to act in the best interests of the Church to prevent errors from being propagated while respecting the rights and stated function of the Catholic theologian.

After a lengthy and eloquent review of the Church's teachings that the "truth which sets us free is a gift of Jesus Christ (cf. Jn 8:32)" and that "Man's deliverance from the alienation of sin and death comes about when Christ, the Truth, becomes the 'way' for him (cf. Jn 14:6)," the instruction notes in very positive terms the function and role of the theologian in the Church. In discussing this role and function, the document echoes the foundational statement by then Father Ratzinger thirty years before when he wrote his famed *Introduction to Christianity*, namely the close relationship between theology and the object of its study. As the instruction declares:

> Among the vocations awakened in this way by the Spirit in the Church is that of the theologian. His role is to pursue in a particular way an ever deeper understanding of the Word of God found in the inspired Scriptures and handed on by the living Tradition of the Church. He does this in communion with

the Magisterium which has been charged with the responsibility of preserving the deposit of faith ... Since the object of theology is the Truth which is the living God and His plan for salvation revealed in Jesus Christ, the theologian is called to deepen his own life of faith and continuously unite his scientific research with prayer.

The Instruction then adds an essential element in the functioning of theology:

> Never forgetting that he is also a member of the People of God, the theologian must foster respect for them and be committed to offering them a teaching which in no way does harm to the doctrine of the faith. The freedom proper to theological research is exercised within the Church's faith. Thus while the theologian might often feel the urge to be daring in his work, this will not bear fruit or "edify" unless it is accompanied by that patience which permits maturation to occur ... Freedom of research, which the academic community rightly holds most precious, means an openness to accepting the truth that emerges at the end of an investigation in which no element has intruded that is foreign to the methodology corresponding to the object under study. In theology this freedom of inquiry is the hallmark of a rational discipline whose object is given by revelation, handed on and interpreted in the Church under the authority of the Magisterium, and received by faith. These givens have the force of principles. To eliminate them would mean to cease doing theology.

The Instruction proceeds to detail the relationship between the theologian and the Magisterium, stating positively that, "The living Magisterium of the Church and theology, while having different gifts and functions, ultimately have the same goal: preserving the People of God in the truth which sets free and thereby making them "a light to the nations." It proceeded by necessity, however, to a thorough discussion of the mandate of the theologian which entails collaboration that "becomes a participation in the work of the Magisterium, linked, as it then is, by a juridic bond." When, therefore, the Magisterium of the Church makes an infallible pronouncement and solemnly declares that a teaching is found in revelation, "the assent called for is that of theological faith."

In order to serve the People of God, the Magisterium "can intervene in questions under discussion which involve, in addition to solid principles, certain contingent and conjectural elements." This leads to a direct discussion of the problem of dissent in the Church. On the issue of dissent, the instruction notes its origins in the ideology of philosophical liberalism which permeates the modern age, the influence of public opinion that can be by manipulated by media to bring pressure to conform, and the plurality of cultures and languages that, while itself a benefit, can indirectly cause misunderstandings. Dissent is commonly defended by various arguments, but two are most common: "The first lies in the order of hermeneutics. The documents of the Magisterium, it is said, reflect nothing more than a debatable theology. The second takes theological pluralism sometimes to the point of a relativism which calls the integrity of the faith into question. Here the interventions of the Magisterium would have their origin in one theology among many theologies, while no particular theology, however, could presume to claim universal normative status."

Finally, the instruction states again the fundamental right and obligation of the Church's Magisterium:

> By virtue of the divine mandate given to it in the Church, the Magisterium has the mission to set forth the Gospel's teaching, guard its integrity, and thereby protect the Faith of the People of God. In order to fulfill this duty, it can at times be led to take serious measures as, for example, when it withdraws from a theologian, who departs from the doctrine of the faith, the canonical mission or the teaching mandate it had given him, or declares that some writings do not conform to this doctrine. When it acts in such ways, the Magisterium seeks to be faithful to its mission of defending the right of the People of God

to receive the message of the Church in its purity and integrity and not be disturbed by a particular dangerous opinion.

As he pondered the difficult job he had held for over twenty years, Cardinal Ratzinger observed in his interview with EWTN that he was grateful for the thanks he had received over the years:

> Also everyday I experience that people are thankful saying, "Yes, the Church has an identity, has a continuity, the faith is real and present also today and is also today possible." And when I go in St. Peter's Square and so on, I can see everyday people from different parts of the world knowing me and saying, "Thank you, Father. We are thankful that you are doing this difficult job, because this is helping us." Even many Protestant friends say to me, "What you are doing is helpful also for us, because it is defending also our faith and the presence of the faith in Christ. We need an instance as yours, even if we are not sharing all that you are saying. But it's also for us helpful to see we have this continuing defense of the faith and this is in encouraging to continue in the faith, and to live it."

The *Catechism of the Catholic Church*

One of the most overlooked accomplishments — of many — on the part of Cardinal Ratzinger during his tenure as Prefect of the CDF was his pivotal role in the organization, drafting, and completion of the *Catechism of the Catholic Church*, the first new collection of Catholic doctrine regarding faith and morals in over four centuries and the release of the famed *Roman Catechism* in 1566. Indeed, Cardinal Ratzinger became one of the key forces in its completion as head of the commission of twelve Cardinals and Bishops charged with the preparation of the draft Catechism. The success of the *Catechism of the Catholic Church* may prove to be one of his life's most lasting achievements.

Pope John Paul II wrote of the development of the Catechism in his 1992 apostolic constitution *Fidei Depositum*. He traced its inception to the Second Vatican Council and its continuing influence upon the Church. In 1985, the pontiff convened an extraordinary assembly of the Synod of Bishops for the 20th anniversary of the close of the Vatican Council. The purpose of the assembly was to celebrate the legacy of the council, including the "graces and spiritual fruits of Vatican II, to study its teaching in greater depth in order that all the Christian faithful might better adhere to it and to promote knowledge and application of it." At the time of the gathering, many bishops expressed a desire for a new catechism or a compendium to have as "a point of reference for the catechisms or compendiums that are prepared in various regions."

From this spontaneous beginning, the Pope consulted with his closest advisors and determined that the time was right for such an undertaking. The following year, the Pope appointed a commission of twelve Cardinals and Bishops, chaired by Cardinal Ratzinger, with the task of preparing a draft of the Catechism. The commission was supported by an editorial committee of seven diocesan Bishops, all experts in theology and catechesis from around the world. Six years of collaboration later, the *Catechism of the Catholic Church* was issued with the joyful approval of the Holy Father.

Cardinal Ratzinger's account of the arduous process was recorded in the *Introduction to the Catechism of the Catholic Church* that he coauthored with then Bishop Christoph (later Cardinal) Schönborn, Auxiliary Bishop of Vienna. Like John Paul II, he documents that the idea for the Catechism originated with the Synod of Bishops in 1985 but that the notion was not an entirely new one. Toward the end of the Second Vatican Council, the German Cardinal Lorenz Jäger of Paderborn had suggested a Catechism to reflect the spirit of *aggiornamento* that the Council intended to inspire in the Church.

Such a project was actually undertaken by the Dutch bishops' conference, and in1966 the famous *Dutch Catechism* was published. Cardinal Ratzinger points out that that catechism was met by an enthusiastic reception, but readers and critics soon raised serious questions, so much so that Pope Paul VI appointed a commission of six Cardinals to investigate its various doctrinal difficulties. The committee lauded its "praiseworthy originality" but cited a number of serious problem areas that needed to be corrected. Then Father Ratzinger wrote in 1968 in the Irish journal *Furrow* in praise of the *Dutch Catechism's* deep religious spirit, but he also noted its various deficiencies, not the least of which was its approach to such fundamental questions as Christology and the Eucharist. The entire affair of the failed experiment of the *Dutch Catechism*, however, raised the question among Catholic educators and members of the Hierarchy as to whether once more some thought should be given to a universal catechism. Ratzinger's opinion at the time was in the negative, as the environment was not yet ready given the state of confusion in the years after the council. He remained firm in this opinion right up to the early 1980s. By then, through the efforts of Pope John Paul II, the post-conciliar atmosphere has matured sufficiently to warrant revisiting the idea. As Cardinal Ratzinger put it in *Introduction to the Catechism of the Catholic Church* (Ignatius, 1994), "In 1966 the full extent of the problem had simply not become visible; that a process of fermentation had just begun which could lead only gradually to the clarifications necessary for a new common word."

In his discussion of catechetics in the years following the Council in the *Introduction to the Catechism of the Catholic Church*, Cardinal Ratzinger recounts a letter he received from a catechist after lectures he had given on the subject in Lyons and Paris. She lamented the fact that she found in class after class that the prevailing method of catechesis of the time was failing in insuring retention by the children. In her experienced opinion, the problem was not with the catechists or the children but with the program itself. It relied upon the most up-to-date methods and materials, but it was sadly empty of content. As Cardinal Ratzinger wrote, "Content had to win back its priority."

Cardinal Ratzinger thus assumed his position as head of the commission for the Catechism, gravely aware of the problem at hand. The first meetings were tense ones, as the members needed to clarify the precise purposes of the Catechism being proposed. The command of the Holy Father was to draft "a plan for a catechism for the whole

Church, or else for a compendium of Catholic doctrine (on faith and morals)." Added to this mandate was that of the Synod participants that the new text be both biblical and liturgical.

The commission, under his leadership, devoted their efforts with remarkable speed and determination over the course of nine drafts and innumerable revisions, emendations, suggestions, and critiques by the bishops of the world as well as theologians, exegetes, and catechists. Pope John Paul II could declare in 1992:

> The project was the object of extensive consultation among all Catholic Bishops, their Episcopal Conferences or Synods, and of theological and catechetical institutes. As a whole, it received a broadly favorable acceptance on the part of the Episcopate. It can be said that this Catechism is the result of the collaboration of the whole Episcopate of the Catholic Church, who generously accepted my invitation to share responsibility for an enterprise which directly concerns the life of the Church. This response elicits in me a deep feeling of joy, because the harmony of so many voices truly expresses what could be called the "symphony" of the faith. The achievement of this Catechism thus reflects the collegial nature of the Episcopate; it testifies to the Church's catholicity.

While he was not solely responsible for the creation of the Catechism, Cardinal Ratzinger was nevertheless head of the committees that were the heart and soul of the process (the original committee for drafting the Catechism and then the Interdicasterial Commission for the *Catechism of the Catholic Church* that led to the publication of the *editio typica*, or official Latin Typical Edition in 1997), and the entire undertaking was a genuinely colossal one involving bishops, experts, and consultors literally from around the planet and representing a host of viewpoints, requirements, perspectives, and cultural sensibilities. Pope John Paul's favorable observation that the Catechism was the result of a collegial activity by those involved was a crucial demonstration of Cardinal Ratzinger's ability to bring together a variety of opinions and personalities and harmonize all of them for the achievement of one goal. As the Cardinal later wrote in *Introduction to the Catechism of the Catholic Church*, (Ignatius Press, 1994):

> The Catechism does not aim to represent the opinions of any one group, but rather the faith of the Church, which is no one's personal invention. Such unity in fundamentals is the indispensable condition of vital plurality. We are already seeing how the Catechism calls forth manifold initiatives; renewed solidarity in a common heritage exists side by side with a new incarnation of this common patrimony in diverse worlds.

Cats and Christmas Cookies

Soon after the conclusion of the conclave that elected Pope Benedict XVI, the American Cardinals who had just taken part held a press conference in Rome at the North American College, the seminary for Americans preparing for the priesthood in Rome. Cardinal Justin Rigali of Philadelphia was asked about his impressions of the new Pope. He said, "We have to be careful about characterizing the Holy Father and very simply putting labels on this man of the Church. He has so many dimensions and so many qualities." The Cardinal added, "As more people get to know this man, and I think the more people know him as we know him, they will love and appreciate him."

The American Cardinals made it clear that the man they had known for a very long time was far from the one who had been portrayed in the media as the stern and humorless head of the department in the Vatican that centuries ago ran the Inquisition. Cardinal Theodore McCarrick of Washington shared Cardinal Rigali's assessment. "The vision that some have of the Holy Father as someone who is not a person of dialogue is a skewed vision," said Cardinal McCarrick. "He's always had a wealth of experience, not just his own, when he comes up with an answer."

As the first days of his pontificate passed, the enormous audiences watching his every move and listening to his every word began to share the opinion of the American members of the College of Cardinals. Pope Benedict's gentleness, humor, and authenticity were made increasingly apparent as his customary shyness and humility were overcome by the enthusiasm of the crowds and the warm reception he received from the people of Rome and the members of the Vatican staff. For those who have known and worked with Joseph Ratzinger, the sudden image of the new Pope was hardly surprising. The personality beheld by the world was the only one they had ever known. Msgr. Lorenzo Albacete wrote on April 24, 2005, in a column for the *New York Daily News* of first meeting the future Pope years after reading the famed *Introduction to Christianity*: "When I first met him, I had expected to find a 'German professor of theology': a serious, austere, imposing, formal man. Instead I found a man made almost transparent by his humility, a man of the most delicate gentility. This impression was there each time I have had the joy of meeting him."

For over two decades, the figure of Cardinal Ratzinger was a fixture in the Eternal City, especially areas around the Vatican City State and the Borgo Pio, and he was famous for walking the streets in a simple black cassock, passing often anonymously through the crowds packing into St. Peter's Square and touring the Vatican and St. Peter's Basilica. Over the years, tourists and pilgrims mistook him for a simple priest in the throng or some cleric serving in the Vatican. They stopped him to ask directions to the Sistine Chapel, what time Masses were held, how the Pope was doing, and when they could see the Holy Father, completely oblivious as to his identity.

Just as many stories have been repeated that for those who recognized him their handshake and compliments were met with a smile, warmth, and appreciation. Seminarians especially sought him out as he headed to work, briefcase in hand, a professor's beret on his head, and wearing his usual black cassock with his high rank only hinted at by the presence of the simple pectoral cross that had hung around his neck since his episcopal consecration in 1977. The students always found him delighted to chat, and he possesses a phenomenal memory for names, home countries, and even what the students were studying.

For most of his time in Rome as a Cardinal, Ratzinger lived in an apartment at the Piazza della Città Leonina, near the final stop for the city's No. 64 bus and not far from the Vatican. His neighbors included two other prominent Cardinals in the Curia, Darío Castrillón Hoyos and Pio Laghi. By custom that only rarely varied, he set out each workday on foot and arrived at the congregation's offices in the Piazza Sant'Uffizio promptly at 9 a.m. The apartment was sparsely decorated save for the one thing that filled the living space — his immense personal library. As one of the nuns who took care of him was heard to comment when he was elected and would be moving into the Apostolic Palace, "He will have to take his library, because he goes nowhere without his library."

When not in Rome, he took his holidays in Austria and various Alpine settings. He was especially fond of hiking in the Tyrol and the northern Italian mountains. As he grew older and the demands of his offices increased, the hiking expeditions declined, and he took to caring for his little house in Regensburg. He thus never lost touch with his beloved Bavaria and his brother. On trips home to Bavaria, he enthusiastically ate traditional local specialties such as Weisswurst (Bavarian sausages) and has always been fond of Christmas cookies of every variety.

Cardinal Ratzinger was also famous in Regensburg for his love of cats and their affection for him. He regularly stopped and said hello to street cats in Regensburg and especially enjoyed playing with kittens who seemed always to find their way to him wherever he might be sitting. As Konrad Baumgartner, the head of the theology department at Regensburg University, recalled in an interview, the two went for a walk in Regensburg and Ratzinger made his way to the old cemetery behind the church. "It was," Baumgartner said, "full of cats, and when he went out, they all ran to him. They knew him and loved him. He stood there, petting some and talking to them, for quite a long time. He visited the cats whenever he visited the church."

In Rome, he is renowned for his courtesy and his abiding culture. He speaks at least four languages fluently, knows a number of others and can read several more. He is fluent in Latin and speaks Italian and English with a southern German accent. He plays the piano and has a fondness for Mozart and Beethoven, but is reluctant to play Brahms as it can be too difficult. His brother Georg remembers that he also played the organ.

Even though he dealt with the highest concerns of the Church and was on a first-name basis with Pope John Paul II and the most powerful figures in the Church, Cardinal Ratzinger was also appreciated for his humble daily routine and for never forgetting the humanity of those with whom he knew or interacted. The American Cardinals attested to his personal kindness. He wished a happy birthday to Cardinal Rigali in the midst of the arduous preparations for the conclave and gave a personal farewell to the future Cardinal Edward Egan when Egan left his job in the Vatican in 1985 and moved back to New York to become an auxiliary bishop under Cardinal John O'Connor. He likewise thanks washroom attendants, makes it a point to greet everyone taking part in a meeting regardless of their rank or importance, and performs great gestures of kindness even if they impede his schedule.

Soon after his election, *Inside the Vatican* reported on the experience of a young German couple, students who had met in Rome on the footsteps of a church and who attended the Mass Cardinal Ratzinger regularly said at the Teutonic church in Vatican City at 7 a.m. for German-speakers. One morning in February 2004, they waited until after Mass and then asked him if he would be willing at all to preside at their wedding. He not only agreed but set aside time to meet with them and prepare them for the sacrament of marriage. He then presided at their wedding Mass in St. Peter's Basilica on June 24, 2004.

Letter of John Paul II to Cardinal Joseph Ratzinger on the 50th Anniversary of His Ordination to the Priesthood

On June 20, 2001, Pope John Paul sent a letter to Cardinal Ratzinger on the 50th anniversary of his ordination to the priesthood. The letter contains a vivid illustration of his close friendship with the pontiff and why he was so valuable a collaborator in the Pope's Petrine ministry.

To my venerable Brother Cardinal Joseph Ratzinger,
Prefect of the Congregation for the Doctrine of the Faith:

With deep joy, Your Eminence, I offer you my warm congratulations and most fervent good wishes on the happy event of the 50th anniversary of your ordination to the priesthood. The coincidence of your Jubilee day with the liturgical solemnity of the Holy Apostles Peter and Paul reminds me of their vision of broad spiritual and ecclesial horizons: personal holiness extended to the supreme sacrifice, missionary outreach combined with constant concern for unity, the necessary integration of spiritual charism and institutional ministry.

These are horizons, Venerable Brother, which you have attentively explored in your theological research: in Peter, the principle of unity is outstanding, founded on faith as firm as the rock of the Princes of the Apostles; in Paul, the need, intrinsic in the Gospel, to call every man and every people to the obedience of faith. Moreover these two dimensions are combined in the common witness of holiness which sealed the generous dedication of the two Apostles to the service of the immaculate Bride of Christ. How can we not also see in these two elements the fundamental features of the path that Providence prepared for you, Your Eminence, in calling you to the priesthood?

Your brilliant philosophical and, in particular, theological studies and your precocious call to teaching roles in the most important German universities should be seen in this perspective of faith. You expressed the intention that has always guided you in your commitment to study and teaching in the motto you chose on the occasion of your episcopal appointment: *Cooperatores veritatis.*

The aim for which you have always striven since your very first years as a priest has been to serve the truth, seeking to know it ever more thoroughly and make it ever more widely known.

It was precisely the consideration of this pastoral aspiration which has constantly marked your academic activity that induced Pope Paul VI of venerable memory to raise you to the episcopal dignity and entrust you with responsibility for the great Archdiocese of München und Freising. It was a crucial transition in your life, which was to give a direction to later developments. Indeed when, shortly afterwards, the unforgettable Pontiff mentioned above created you a Cardinal, you found yourself directly bound to collaborating with the Apostolic See. Twenty years ago I asked you to collaborate full time as Prefect of the Congregation for the Doctrine of the Faith. Since then you have not ceased to expend your intellectual and moral energies in promoting and protecting the doctrine of the faith and its morals throughout the Catholic world (cf. Apostolic Constitution *Pastor Bonus,* n. 48), while encouraging studies aimed at increasing knowledge of the faith so that the new problems arising from the progress of science and civilization could be conveniently answered in the light of the Word of God (cf. *ibid.,* n. 49).

In this office, Your Eminence, the Apostles Peter and Paul have inspired your priestly life and your ecclesial service further and in the loftiest way. This happy event is a favourable opportunity for me to reiterate my deep gratitude to you for the impressive volume of work you have carried out and directed in the dicastery entrusted to you, and even more, for the spirit of humility and self-denial that has constantly marked your activity. May the Lord lavish his rewards upon you!

On this occasion which is so significant for you, I would like to tell you that the spiritual communion you have always shown with regard to the Successor of Peter has been a great comfort to me in the daily effort of my service to Christ and to the Church. I therefore pray the Lord, through the intercession of the Blessed Virgin Mary, for the choicest heavenly favours for you, for your ministry and for all your loved ones, as I impart a special heartfelt Apostolic Blessing to you with a fraternal sentiment of affection.   JOHN PAUL II

Above all, he is a man of intense prayer who since his childhood has understood that the Eucharist is the source and summit of the Christian life, as the Second Vatican Council proclaimed. It is noted that he uses any spare moments during his routine of the day to recite the breviary, sometimes ducking away during conferences and symposia to pray in empty rooms or anywhere that a fleeting moment of solitude will permit. Regarding the Mass, Cardinal Ratzinger authored entire books on the subject of the Eucharist and the Liturgy. of the Eucharist, he wrote in 2003 in *A God Who Is Near*:

> Although we are the ones who caused the conflict, and although God was not the culprit, but us, it is he who comes to meet us and who, in Christ, begs for reconciliation. The more we walk with him the more conscious we are that the God who seems to torment us is the one who really loves us and is the one to whom we can abandon ourselves without resistance or fear. The more we enter into the night of the misunderstood mystery the more we trust him, the more we find him, the more we discover the love and freedom that sustain us through all the nights. God gives so that we can give. This is the essence of the eucharistic sacrifice, of the sacrifice of Jesus Christ.

As for his own view of himself, Cardinal Ratzinger is characteristically reticent. In an interview in 2001, he was asked to describe himself and replied with some reluctance. In the end, he declared:

> It is impossible to paint a self-portrait; it is difficult to judge oneself. I can only say that I come from a very simple family, very humble, and that is why I feel more like a simple man than a Cardinal. I have my home in Germany, in a small village, with people who work in agriculture, in craftsmanship, and there I feel at home. I also try to be like this in my work: I don't know if I succeed, I don't dare judge myself. I always remember very affectionately the profound goodness of my father and my mother and, naturally, for me, goodness means

the capacity to say "no," because a goodness that allows everything does the other no good. At times goodness means having to say "no," and run the risk of contradiction. These are my criteria, this is my origin; the rest must be judged by others.

Chapter 9

LET US MOVE FORWARD
✠

Let us move forward in the joy of the Risen Lord, confident of his unfailing help! The Lord will help us, and Mary, his Most Holy Mother, will be on our side.

— POPE BENEDICT XVI

The Future

On the morning of April 20, barely twelve hours after his stunning election as successor to John Paul II, Pope Benedict XVI celebrated Mass with the College of Cardinals in the Sistine Chapel. Beyond the powerful symbolism in the gathering, the Mass was significant for offering the new pontiff the opportunity to give his first address as Pope. The address was a remarkable moment, for in the span of only a few paragraphs, the new Pope provided a clear glimpse into the priorities of his pontificate. He proclaimed immediately, "I undertake this special ministry, the 'Petrine' ministry at the service of the Universal Church, with humble abandon to the hands of the Providence of God. And it is to Christ in the first place that I renew my total and trustworthy adhesion."

Pope Benedict XVI assumes the papacy with a breadth of knowledge of the global situation in the Church that is matched by his long years of experience as Prefect of the Congregation for the Doctrine of the Faith. By necessity, his long toils as prefect involved him in virtually every pastoral and doctrinal undertaking of the previous pontificate. Such a treasury of personal resources will be invaluable to the Pope as he begins to grapple with the issues, crises, and opportunities confronting the Church at the start of the third millennium. Additionally, Pope Benedict XVI will have his own priorities as his pontificate is firmly established. These were enumerated to some degree in his address in the Sistine Chapel to the College of Cardinals and included a stress upon unity, collegiality, outreach to the other Christian denominations and world religions, and the young.

Chapter 3 of this book, concerning the issues facing the Cardinals as they entered the conclave, reviewed these very priorities. The topics revealed the enormity of the task that lies ahead for Pope Benedict XVI and included seven key concerns:

- The decline of faith, particularly in Europe with its direct challenge to the central place of Christ and basic belief in God.
- The challenges facing the Church in the Third World.
- The challenge of interreligious dialogue with Islam, Judaism, and other world religions and ecumenism with the other Christian denominations.
- Issues of Church governance, the relationship between the particular churches and the Universal Church, and controversial topics in the Church *ad intra*.
- Liturgical renewal.
- The ecclesial movements.
- The challenge of youth and the road to the future.

This list makes no claim to be an exhaustive one, nor is there an effort here to predict what the Pope will do or to suggest in any way a course of action — such a right is his alone to execute as he sees fit, according to Church law and teaching. Rather, the issues are seen in light of then Cardinal Ratzinger's comments and writings and his statements since his election. This might serve to glean a sense of how he will perhaps view them as his pontificate unfolds.

The Crisis of Faith in the First World

By nearly unanimous opinion, the Cardinal Electors expressed grave concerns for the state of culture and faith in the First World.

The impact of this dilemma touches upon every aspect of life, including the progress of the Church in reaching out to the modern world and proclaiming the Gospel. Cardinal Tarcisio Bertone of Genoa, who had worked with then Cardinal Ratzinger for seven years as Secretary for the Congregation for the Doctrine of the Faith from 1995 to 2002, stated plainly in an interview with Vatican radio where he saw the central priority for the new pontificate rested:

> I believe that we must not give up and that Benedict XVI will guide us in the work of refounding our culture, the life of our society, of our nations, on the Judeo-Christian roots and, therefore, we will also be able to see a flowering of testimonies, namely of those who demonstrate how it is possible to live according to our Christian roots. There are so many who want this. So many who follow the Pope.

For Cardinal Bertone, the task in its practical implementation is a twofold one. First, there is the necessity of proclaiming the Gospel, the New Evangelization. Second, the Church under Pope Benedict must meet the pressing challenge to implement the Second Vatican Council, in fidelity to the 2,000-year tradition of the Church. The new Pope, he noted, has been ideally placed for the accomplishment of both over the last years. "Cardinal Ratzinger got us accustomed to, educated us to give reasons for our faith; a clear Christian identity in order to dialogue with everyone. It is necessary to begin from an understanding and a testimony of one's own identity of faith, with respect for all, proposing and not imposing, as he has always done in his dialogue with dissidents."

As a theologian and a Cardinal, Pope Benedict returned again and again to the theme of relativism as a genuine calamity for contemporary culture and the Catholic faith and one that influences every facet of the world today. Though attacked by critics for being a "*sturm und drang*" diatribe against the modern world, then Cardinal's Ratzinger's homily on the morning of the conclave was a masterpiece of clarity in explaining the problem of our age. Our goal must be to be "adults in the faith" and not "children in a state of guardianship, tossed about by the waves and carried here and there by every wind of doctrine." This demand is all the more urgent because the times are plunging forward into "a dictatorship of relativism which recognizes nothing as definitive and leaves as the ultimate standard one's own personality and desires."

For the Christian, relativism is matched and overcome by an entirely different standard of living, Jesus Christ. Christ is the standard for "true humanism" and "the criterion for discerning between the true and the false, between deception and truth." We must also have the courage to proclaim the truth, to stand up to a culture that declares the proclamation of the Gospel to be religious fundamentalism.

The practical effects of relativism are visible in Western society in a host of ways: the destruction of objective morality; the promotion of abortion, homosexual acts, and euthanasia as reflections of the absence of universal norms of conduct; secularization and de-Christianization in the name of pluralism, as seen with the drafting of the European Union's new Constitution that excised any mention of the Christian roots of modern Europe; and the proliferation of the New Age movement and the embrace by men and women of pagan religions as a rejection of the Judaeo-Christian heritage of Europe. In the Church, relativism is visible in the push to apply modern forms of democratic thinking to Church governance and to loosen Church teachings to conform to the current sexual mores of society instead of adhering to the unchanging truths of the Catholic faith.

The relativist position would suggest that anyone who understands and asserts in modern society that there are objective truths is intolerant and therefore should be silenced in the name of subjective truth and a pluralistic society. The result of this outlook is to bring the very dictatorship Cardinal Ratzinger warned about in his homily before the conclave. What is more, relativism is inherently destructive to the social order for it tears away the essential things that all people have in common. As he puts it, "If we cannot have common values, common truths, sufficient communication on the essentials of human life — how to live, how to respond to the great challenges of human life — then true society becomes impossible."

Cardinal Ratzinger in 1998 gave a powerful answer to the understandable question of how the Church should respond to the demonstrable predicament in the West. His vision is for the Catholic faith not to withdraw into itself, into closed groups. Instead, it must reach out to address and to enlighten everyone. The model for this action is the Church in the first centuries when the population of Christians were few. Despite their limited numbers, they came to the attention of all because they were not closed off. They challenged the culture of their time and lived with a sense of universal mission. So, too, do the Catholics in a post-modern world have the same mission as our brothers and sisters nearly two thousand years ago: "to make present the real answer to the demand of a life that corresponds to the Creator."

The Challenges for the Church in the Southern Hemisphere

There is little question that the population centers of the Church have definitively shifted to the Southern Hemisphere where 700 million Catholics live, in particular in Latin America where there are over 450 million Catholics. The issues facing the Church in those regions are daunting ones as was documented in the chapter on the conclave. Pope Benedict XVI has not been ignorant of these challenges. Rather, he has been in the forefront of the effort to advance the authentic teachings of the Church as the solution to these needs and problems. In an address given on March 18, 2005, only weeks before his election, then Cardinal Ratzinger celebrated the 40th anniversary of the Second Vatican Council document *Gaudium et Spes*, on the Church in the Modern World. He spoke directly of the issues of social justice and the Church's mission in the world:

> As Christians we must constantly be reminded that the call of justice is not something which can be reduced to the categories of this world. And this is the beauty of the Pastoral

Constitution *Gaudium et Spes,* evident in the very structure of the Council's text; only when we Christians grasp our vocation, as having been created in the image of God and believing that "the form of this world is passing away... [and] that God is preparing a new dwelling and a new earth, in which justice dwells" (*Gaudium et Spes,* n. 39), can we address the urgent social problems of our time from a truly Christian perspective. "Far from diminishing our concern to develop this earth, the expectation of a new earth should spur us on, for it is here that the body of a new human family grows, prefiguring in some way the world that is to come" (*ibid.,* n. 39).

And so, the Cardinal insists, "to be workers of this true justice, we must be workers who are *being made just* by contact with him who is justice itself: Jesus of Nazareth. The place of this encounter is the Church, nowhere more powerfully present than in her sacraments and liturgy."

This is not a vague or overly spiritualized approach to solving the problems of the developing world, but a profound commentary on the true mission of the Church. This truth was underscored earlier in the homily when he said:

> It is certainly true that today, when the Church commits herself to works of justice on a human level (and there are few institutions in the world which accomplish what the Catholic Church accomplishes for the poor and disadvantaged), the world praises the Church. But when the Church's work for justice touches on issues and problems which the world no longer sees as bound up with human dignity, like protecting the right to life of every human being from conception to natural death, or when the Church confesses that justice also includes our responsibilities toward God himself, then the world not infrequently reaches for the stones mentioned in our Gospel today.

Cardinal Ratzinger's concern for the true implementation of justice raised one other crucial point, namely the Church's proclamation of justice. Classical theology understands the virtue of justice to be composed of two inseparable elements: justice as the will to render to God what is owed to God, and to render to our neighbor what is owed to him. As such, Cardinal Ratzinger reminded his listeners, "justice toward other human beings is the fundamental attitude that respects the other as a person created by God."

As was followed in the chapter detailing Cardinal Ratzinger's labors as Prefect of the Congregation for the Doctrine of the Faith, he famously grappled with the issue of Liberation Theology in the 1980s. His efforts, in answering the concerns of Pope John Paul II to proclaim authentic teachings, helped significantly to reorient the efforts at liberation in light of the Gospels. Cardinal Ratzinger spoke of the issue of liberation as it relates directly to the developing world in a meeting of the Congregation for the Doctrine of the Faith with the presidents of the Doctrinal Commissions of the Bishops' Conferences of Latin America, held in Guadalajara, Mexico, in May 1996:

> We experience a world that does not correspond to a good God. Poverty, oppression, all kinds of unjust domination, the suffering of the just and the innocent constitute the signs of the times and of all times. And we all suffer: No one can readily say to this world and to his or her own life, "Stay as you are, you are so beautiful."
>
> From this the theology of liberation deduced that the situation, which must not continue, could only be overcome through a radical change in the structures of this world which are structures of sin and evil. If sin exerts its power over the structures and impoverishment is programmed beforehand by them, then its overthrow cannot come about through individual conversions, but through the struggle against the structures of injustice. It was said, however, that this struggle ought to be political because the structures are consolidated and preserved through politics. Redemption thus became a political process for which the Marxist philosophy provided the essential guide-

lines. It was transformed into a task which people themselves could and even had to take into their own hands, and at the same time it became a totally practical hope: Faith, in theory, became praxis, concrete redeeming action, in the process of liberation.

The collapse of the Soviet Union and the subsequent decline of the extreme forms of Liberation Theology in Latin America demonstrated the validity of Cardinal Ratzinger's views. As he put it, "The non-fulfillment of this hope [of liberation and redemption] brought a great disillusionment with it which is still far from being assimilated . . . The failure of the only scientifically based system for solving human problems could only justify nihilism or, in any case, total relativism." In this way, the challenges facing the developing world are tied to the same overarching concerns of the civilization of the West — relativism and its many manifestations — that are seen by Pope Benedict as the central problem for the faith at the present time.

That the tribulations facing the developing world are, indeed, on the mind of the new Pope was seen in his address in the Sistine Chapel. But his concern flows, as did that of Pope John Paul II, from the source of hope for the world:

> The Eucharist makes the Risen Christ constantly present, Christ Who continues to give Himself to us, calling us to participate in the banquet of His Body and His Blood. From this full communion with Him comes every other element of the life of the Church, in the first place the communion among the faithful, the commitment to proclaim and give witness to the Gospel, the ardor of charity towards all, especially towards the poor and the smallest.

Ecumenism and Interreligious Dialogue

A firestorm of controversy surrounded the publication in 2000 of the declaration *Dominus Iesus* by the Congregation for the Doctrine of the Faith, with dire predictions made at the time that the very presence of the document would set back dialogue with both other Christian denominations and the world's religions. With the election of Cardinal Ratzinger as Pope Benedict XVI, the question was raised immediately as to how he would proceed with the outreach to other believers and other faiths that had been a hallmark of the Wojtylan pontificate.

As was seen with the true purpose of *Dominus Iesus*, Cardinal Ratzinger assisted the Church in understanding the genuine Catholic position regarding the "Unicity and Salvific Universality of Jesus Christ and the Church" and to discern the opportunities and risks that dialogue brings as the Church reaches out to other religions and denominations. Rather than discouraging dialogue, the document served to clarify the Church's teachings for all Catholics so that they might have a firmer foundation for authentic and meaningful discourse. As he stated in an interview in 2002:

> Christ is totally different from all the founders of other religions, and he cannot be reduced to a Buddha, a Socrates or a Confucius. He is really the bridge between heaven and earth, the light of truth who has appeared to us.
>
> The gift of knowing Jesus does not mean that there are no important fragments of truth in other religions. In the light of Christ, we can establish a fruitful dialogue with a point of reference in which we can see how all these fragments of truth contribute to greater depth in our faith and to an authentic spiritual community of humanity. I would say that at the present time the dialogue with the other religions is the most important point: to understand how, on one hand, Christ is unique, and on the other, how he answers all others, who are precursors of Christ, and who are in dialogue with Christ.

Pope Benedict XVI wasted no time in placing himself firmly and unhesitatingly in the tradition of his predecessor in the Church's commitment to dialogue. On April 25, in the Sala Clementina in the Apostolic Palace, the Pope received the representatives of Christian denominations and other religions who had attended the Mass for the solemn inauguration of his pontificate the day before. He stated in an address that he was committed to the Church's "irreversible" effort at ecumenism. He then spoke in two parts to his audience. The first was aimed at the delegates of the various Orthodox Churches, the Eastern Orthodox Churches, and the ecclesial communities of the West, namely the Protestant denominations. The second was directed to the representatives of other religions.

In speaking to the ecclesial communities of the West, Pope Benedict declared: "Following in the footsteps of my predecessors, in particular Paul VI and John Paul II, I feel intensely the need to affirm again the irreversible commitment assumed by Vatican Council II to journey on the 'path toward the full communion desired by Jesus for his disciples.'" He then added that the task

> ... implies a concrete docility to what the Spirit says to the churches, courage; gentleness; firmness; and hope, to reach the end. It implies, above all, insistent prayer and, with only one heart, to obtain from the Good Shepherd the gift of unity for his flock. On this very particular occasion, which brings us together precisely at the beginning of my ecclesial service, accepted with fear and confident obedience to the Lord, I ask all of you that you give example with me of that spiritual ecumenism, which in prayer realizes our communion without obstacles.

That progress is possible in the area of Ecumenism with both the Orthodox Churches and the various Protestant denominations is attested by the statements of various leaders in those ecclesial communities. Dr. Rowan Williams, the Anglican Archbishop of Canterbury, attended the solemn inauguration of the Pope, the first leader of the Anglican Communion to do so since the Protestant Reformation. He took part in the gathering in the Clementine Hall and made a revealing public statement afterward. "What has encouraged us on this visit is two things," Dr. Williams said. "One is that, of course,

Pope Benedict has gone out of his way to underline his sense of the priority of ecumenical work. He has spoken of being servants of unity, and we have taken that very much to heart as we have listened."

Dr. Williams continues, "But the second theme, which I think came through very clearly in the magnificent homily he preached at the inaugural Mass, was a theme of united Christian witness, a witness to the fact that — as he said in that homily — 'the Gospel does not ask us to become less than human but more deeply human.'"

The Archbishop of Canterbury also extended an invitation to Pope Benedict to visit England "and to get to know the Church of England whenever that is possible." He concluded by suggesting:

> It seems to me that the events of recent weeks, the death and the funeral of John Paul II and the events around the inauguration of this weekend, have shown a kind of foretaste of a worldwide fellowship of people gathered for worship in a way that has somehow gone around the difficulties of doctrinal definition. It is as if we have been given a glimpse of other levels of unity, and my own feeling is that is the level at which he will seek to work. That is certainly my prayer.

How relations will proceed with the Orthodox Churches is impossible to tell given the many unresolved differences and the continued intransigence of the Russian Orthodox Patriarch of Moscow Alexy II. Nevertheless, Alexy II offered hope for the future when he said:

> Our Churches, which have authority and influence, should unite their efforts to spread Christian values to modern humankind. The secular world is losing its spiritual way and needs our joint testimony as never before.

Pope Benedict XVI has pledged a continuation of ecumenical dialogue with the promise of making genuine progress in that regard. Most apparent is that a rapprochement with the Orthodox could be a genuine possibility in this pontificate as the leadership of the

Orthodox communities finds increasing solidarity with Rome over the pressing problems of relativism and de-Christianization that are spreading across Europe.

Pope Benedict also paid special attention to the representatives of other religions, offering "warm and affectionate greetings to you and to all those who belong to the religions that you represent. I assure you that the Church wants to continue building bridges of friendship with the followers of all religions, in order to seek the true good of every person and of society as a whole."

As the last years have witnessed, three primary concerns in the area of Interreligious Dialogue have been the interaction of the Church with Islam, the cleansing of memory in the Church's relationship with Judaism, and the dealings between a missionary Church in Asia and the ancient religions of those regions, most notably Buddhism and Hinduism.

The new pontiff is well aware of the necessity to differentiate between moderate Muslims and Islamist extremists who have transformed their religion into an ideological weapon for the promotion of global jihad, the destruction of the West, and the persecution of Christians in predominantly Islamic countries. Great progress was made under Pope John Paul II in dialogue with Islam, and Benedict renewed the Church's promise "for the growth of dialogue between Muslims and Christians, both at the local and international level."

Noting the international events that currently dominate the relations between the West and Islam, Benedict returned the conversation to the one that proved so fruitful under John Paul II — the call for peace:

> The world in which we live is often marked by conflicts, violence and war, but it earnestly longs for peace, peace which is above all a gift from God, peace for which we must pray without ceasing. Yet peace is also a duty to which all peoples must be committed, especially those who profess to belong to religious traditions. Our efforts to come together and foster dialogue are a valuable contribution to building peace on solid

foundations. Pope John Paul II, my venerable predecessor, wrote at the start of the new millennium that "the name of the one God must become increasingly what it is: a name of peace and a summons to peace" (*Novo Millennio Ineunte*, 55). It is therefore imperative to engage in authentic and sincere dialogue, built on respect for the dignity of every human person, created, as we Christians firmly believe, in the image and likeness of God (cf. Gen 1:26-27).

Despite the minor controversy that erupted in the few days after his election regarding his enforced membership in the Hitler Youth and his brief mandatory service in the German Army at the end of World War II, the election of Benedict XVI was greeted very warmly by members of the Jewish faith. Abraham H. Foxman, Anti-Defamation League National Director, for example, said in a statement, "He has shown this sensitivity countless times, in meetings with Jewish leadership and in important statements condemning anti-Semitism and expressing profound sorrow for the Holocaust."

The record of the new Pope in this area is an especially strong one. As head of the CDF and also as president of the International Theological Commission and Pontifical Biblical Commission, Cardinal Ratzinger was heavily involved in several key documents, including "Memory and Reconciliation," the 1999 a document that expressed regret for the actions of some of the Church's members toward Jews over the centuries, and especially "The Jewish People and Their Sacred Scriptures in the Christian Bible," a 205-page report prepared by the Pontifical Biblical Commission that was seen as a source for fruitful dialogue with the Jewish people over the "inexhaustible riches" of our shared sacred texts and expressed regret for the improper use of certain Scriptural passages as a means of justifying anti-Semitism.

Cardinal Ratzinger also authored a very widely-read and appreciated Christmas reflection in December 2000 that was published in *L'Osservatore Romano*, the official newspaper of the Holy See. He wrote, "Even if the most recent, loathsome experience of the Shoah [Holocaust] was perpetrated in the name of an anti-Christian ideology, which tried to strike the Christian faith at its Abrahamic roots in the people of Israel, it cannot be denied that a certain insufficient resistance to this atrocity on the part of Christians can be explained by an inherited anti-Judaism present in the hearts of not a few Christians."

With regard to the religions of Asia, Pope Benedict will deal with the pressures in India and elsewhere for Catholics to compromise in the Faith to deal with other religions or to embrace syncretism in the name of dialogue. While encouraging genuine discourse, Cardinal Ratzinger spoke in 1996 of the dangers of lapsing into relativism. Christian theology in India, he warns, might be tempted to "set aside the image of Christ from its exclusive position—which is considered typically Western—in order to place it on the same level as the Indian saving myths. The historical Jesus—it is now thought—is no more the absolute Logos than any other saving figure of history." The very concern about confusion among the faithful in fact led to the notification in 1997 by the CDF that the writings of the Indian Jesuit priest Father Anthony de Mello (died 1987) were incompatible with the Catholic faith, because of his presentation of God as a "cosmic reality, vague and omnipresent" and Jesus not as "the Son of God, but simply as the one who teaches us that all people are children of God."

Controversies in the Church

The Western media place great focus on the issues the Church faces *ad intra*, that is, in the internal life of the faith, such as the continuing financial fallout of the sex-abuse scandals, controversies pertaining to the call from some for the ordination of women and an end to priestly celibacy, and the widespread phenomenon of ongoing dissent over contraception, abortion, homosexual acts, divorce, and bioethical issues (cloning, embryonic stem cell research, etc.). In a broad sense, Cardinal Ratzinger attributed many of these issues to relativist tendencies and the wider crisis of faith among some of the Christian faithful. He said in 1996:

The abandonment of the faith by many is based on the fact that it seems to them that the faith should be decided by some requests, which would be like a kind of party program: Whoever has power decides what must be part of the faith. Therefore, it is important within the Church itself to arrive at power or, on the contrary—which is more logical and obvious—to not believe.

The solution as he has proposed it throughout his career as a priest, theologian, and bishop has been for ongoing catechesis of the faithful and fidelity to the renewal of the Church called for by the Second Vatican Council. Rather than being opposed to dialogue, he used his address in the Sistine Chapel to declare exactly the opposite:

> Theological dialogue is necessary. A profound examination of the historical reasons behind past choices is also indispensable. But even more urgent is that "purification of memory," which was so often evoked by John Paul II, and which alone can dispose souls to welcome the full truth of Christ. It is before Him, supreme Judge of all living things, that each of us must stand, in the awareness that one day we must explain to Him what we did and what we did not do for the great good that is the full and visible unity of all His disciples.

On the matter of Collegiality, or the way in which the Bishops of the Church are united under the Pope as an episcopal community, Cardinal Ratzinger wrote on the question of whether collegiality should operate at the level of the governance of the Universal Church that "Individual bishops share in the government of the universal Church not by being represented in some central organ but by leading as shepherds over their particular Churches which together form and carry in themselves the whole Church . . . It is in governing the particular Church that the bishops share in governing the universal Church." As Pope, Benedict also reiterated, "This collegial communion, even in the diversity of roles and functions of the Supreme Pontiff and the bishops, is at the service of the Church and the unity of faith, from which depends in a notable measure the effectiveness of the evangelizing action of the contemporary world."

Regarding the ordination of women, Cardinal Ratzinger was actively engaged as head of the CDF in explaining the Church's inability to ordain women to the priesthood. When in the wake of Pope John Paul II's 1994 apostolic letter *Ordinatio Sacerdotalis* ("Priestly Ordination"), the question was raised by a bishop's inquiry as to how the term "definitively held" should be understood as it pertained to the declaration "that the Church has no authority whatsoever to confer priestly ordination on women," the response was issued on October 28, 1995, under Cardinal Ratzinger's signature: "This teaching requires definitive assent, since, founded on the written Word of God and from the beginning constantly preserved and applied in the Tradition of the Church, it has been set forth infallibly by the ordinary and universal Magisterium (cf. Second Vatican Council, Dogmatic Constitution on the Church *Lumen Gentium*, 25, 2)." Likewise, concerning the possible ordination of women to the diaconate, the International Theological Commission in 2002 concluded that the permanent diaconate belongs to the sacrament of orders and thus is limited to men only. In his commentary to *Ordinatio Sacerdotalis*, Cardinal Ratzinger wrote:

> The Pope's intervention was necessary, not simply to reiterate the validity of a discipline observed in the Church from the beginning, but to confirm a doctrine "preserved by the constant and universal Tradition of the Church and firmly taught by the Magisterium in its more recent documents," which "pertains to the Church's divine constitution itself" (n. 4). In this way, the Holy Father intended to make clear that the teaching that priestly ordination is to be reserved solely to men could not be considered "open to debate" and neither could one attribute to the decision of the Church "a merely disciplinary force" (*ibid.*). . . . Furthermore, to understand that this teaching implies no injustice or discrimination against women, one has to consider the nature of the ministerial priesthood itself, which

is a service and not a position of privilege or human power over others. Whoever, man or woman, conceives of the priesthood in terms of personal affirmation, as a goal or point of departure in a career of human success, is profoundly mistaken, for the true meaning of Christian priesthood, whether it be the common priesthood of the faithful or, in a most special way, the ministerial priesthood, can only be found in the sacrifice of one's own being in union with Christ, in service of the brethren. Priestly ministry constitutes neither the universal ideal nor even less, the goal of Christian life. In this connection, it is helpful to recall once again that "the only higher gift, which can and must be desired, is charity" (cf. 1 Cor 13:13; *Inter insigniores*, VI).

The new Pope has been equally clear in his frequent examination of the great moral issues of our time and the emergence of what John Paul II classically called the culture of death. He sees these matters as did his predecessor as relating directly to the dignity of the human person: "Where man is no longer seen as one who is under the particular protection of God, there begins the barbarism which tramples on humanity. Where the sense of the singular dignity of each person, in the light of God's design, is lost, there the project of mankind is horribly deformed, and his freedom, devoid of rule, becomes monstrous." He has eloquently opposed abortion and euthanasia, and sees such scientific activities as cloning to be an act of arrogance in that we may strive to "conquer death by our own efforts, yet in reality we are profoundly debasing human dignity."

In 2002, Cardinal Ratzinger expressed his dismay that there has been a tendency to be "too concerned with ourselves, with structural questions, with celibacy, the ordination of women, pastoral councils, the rights of these councils [and] of synods." Instead, the focus must be on helping a world that is desperate and thirsting for answers and does not know how to live. "This," he argued, "is a fundamental point: We must make the Gospel accessible to today's secularized world."

Liturgical Renewal

From his first encounters with the glories of the Mass as a young boy in Bavaria, Benedict XVI has been in love with the liturgy and has focused much theological energy to its study, appreciation, and proper implementation. He was a supporter of the ideals of the liturgical renewal that were launched by the Second Vatican Council, but he has also long been an outspoken adherent of a "reform of the reform" to bring liturgical renewal into full compliance and fidelity with the Council. As he was quoted as saying in 1984 in *L'Osservatore Romano*:

> Certainly, the results [of Vatican II] seem cruelly opposed to the expectations of everyone, beginning with those of Pope John XXIII and then of Paul VI: expected was a new Catholic unity and instead we have been exposed to a dissension which — to use the words of Pope Paul VI — seems to have gone from self-criticism to self-destruction. Expected was a new enthusiasm, and many wound up discouraged and bored. Expected was a great step forward, and instead we find ourselves faced with a progressive process of decadence which had developed for the most part precisely under the sign of a calling back to the Council, and has therefore contributed to discrediting it for many.

The results of this failed implementation have been documented in his writings and speeches. He points, for example, to the excessive creative freedoms that were used in the wake of the new *Ordo Missae*; the extreme differences between the liturgies celebrated in different places according to the new books; the need for those communities that love the old liturgy to be fully integrated into the life of the Church; and the necessity to teach the faithful that orthodox forms of a rite "are the expressions of the life of the Church in which are condensed the faith, the prayer and the very life of generations, and in which are incarnated in a concrete form at once the action of God and the response of man." Liturgy is itself not separate from the Church's many other activities; it is at the center of them. Therefore the liturgy must be what Cardinal Ratzinger termed "living catechesis." He gave a general sense of a solution in his EWTN interview in 2003:

> I think we have to restore not so much certain ceremonies, but the essential idea of liturgy — to understand in liturgy, we are not representing ourselves, but we receive the grace of the presence of the Lord with the Church of the heaven and of the earth. And the universality of the liturgy, it seems to me, is essential. Definition of liturgy and restoring this idea would also help to be more obedient to the norms, not as a juridical positivism, but really as sharing, participating in what is given to us from the Lord in the Church.

Ecclesial Movements

On May 30, 1998, the city of Rome witnessed one of the largest gatherings in its history, and one of the most massive assemblies in the long pontificate of John Paul II. Over 500,000 men, women, and children packed into St. Peter's Square and soon flowed down the Via della Conciliazione and past the Tiber River beyond. The occasion was the enormous outdoor Mass celebrated by the Pope for the ecclesial movements of the Church. Members of 56 different Church movements overwhelmed Rome and St. Peter's Square to express their enthusiasm, their spiritual strength, and their commitment to John Paul II. Among the movements represented were Focolare, the Neocatechumenal Way, L'Arche, and Communion and Liberation. The Pope told the exuberant crowd, "The Spirit is always awesome whenever he intervenes. He arouses astonishing new events; he radically changes people and history."

The emergence of ecclesial movements has been one of the most notable developments on the Church following the Second Vatican Council. The process has witnessed the flowering of such movements as Foclolare founded by Chiara Lubich and Communion and Liberation by Luigi Giussani. As Cardinal Christoph Schönborn reminded the gathering in Rome, such movements have manifested themselves in the Church's history since Pentecost and have increased in numbers since the Council. Cardinal Schönborn also took note of the potential problems faced by such movements, as they are complex realities where the spiritual and secular meet and in which problems can develop. The movements encounter poor relations at times with local dioceses and parishes and run the risk of becoming "churches within the Church" or assuming control over those activities properly within the purview of parishes.

As part of the celebrations in 1998, Cardinal Ratzinger gave the opening address at a three-day conference, "Ecclesial Movements: Communion and Mission on the Threshold of the Third Millennium." He spoke directly of the period after the Council, called a "winter" for the Church, and the sudden way that the Holy Spirit "once again asked for the floor, so to speak." Movements, he said, experience childhood illnesses such as an extreme exclusivity and a failure to become part of the Catholic community. They might also succumb to the temptation of "identifying themselves with the Church herself." At the same time, Cardinal Ratzinger cautioned pastors and bishops to cooperate with the movements. Bishops, he urged, should "have the task of discernment in order to help the movements find the right path for peaceful unity, and to help the parish priests to open themselves and allow themselves to be surprised by these ways inspired by the Spirit." Parish priests should remember that it is "necessary to safeguard the unity of the faithful, who are one single Church and not many churches. It is very important to be very aware of being part of one single Church, in such a way that the phenomena that arise are at the service of the one Church in which everyone has a place."

For the new pontiff, the ecclesial movements provide a valuable means of transforming culture in a world in dire need of the Gospel. He has personal memories of encountering the movements as they were first established, such as the Neo-Catechumens, who emphasized baptism "at a time when families and schools were not initiating people into the faith." He first came to know Communion and Liberation at the end of the 1960s when Msgr. Giussani and his people were offering an alternative to the Marxist revolutionaries in Italy — "a fresher and more radical revolution: the Christian faith." The movements will play a part in the resurrection of Christian culture in the West as clearly envisioned by the new pontiff. As Cardinal Ratzinger put it in 1998, "The Gospel is for everyone and the movements can be of great help, because they have the missionary impulse of the early times, even in the smallness of their numbers, and they can give impetus to the life of the Gospel in the world."

The Challenge of Youth and the Road to the Future

In his address to the Cardinals in the Sistine Chapel, Pope Benedict pointed to a reality in the Church today: the Church left behind by John Paul II "is more courageous, freer, younger. A Church that, according to his teaching and example, looks with serenity to the past and is not afraid of the future." The connection between John Paul II and the young around the world was both remarkable and one of the great resources for the future of the Church. Indeed, millions of young people consider themselves today the John Paul II Generation, a reflection both of the way that the deceased pontiff had deeply touched their lives at a time when they were maturing in the Catholic faith and of the simple fact that for any Catholic under the age of thirty, John Paul II was the only Pope they have ever known.

That Pope Benedict spoke directly to those young and active Catholics in the first major address of his pontificate indicates the degree of his own commitment to them as their shepherd. He declared in the Sistine Chapel that he was already anticipating his first major trip as pontiff, in August to Cologne, Germany. The journey will not only be to his homeland, it will have the specific purpose of celebrating with hundreds of thousands of young people at the World Youth Day:

> I am particularly thinking of young people. To them, the
> privileged interlocutors of John Paul II, I send an affectionate

embrace in the hope, God willing, of meeting them at Cologne on the occasion of the next World Youth Day. With you, dear young people, I will continue to maintain a dialogue, listening to your expectations in an attempt to help you meet ever more profoundly the living, ever young, Christ.

The Pope understands as well that the Catholic Church's future rests in the hand of the young. The exuberance and commitment of the young Catholics who will gather in Cologne point to that promise of the coming years. There seems at first glance little reason for optimism. Pope Benedict sees with greater clarity than any other Church leader the same two interconnected worlds pondered by the Cardinal Electors as they entered into the conclave. Two worlds woven together by the labors of the Church but plagued by the dilemmas of the age that afflict the richest with loneliness and spiritual hunger in the midst of prosperity in the great cities of New York, London, and Paris and the poorest of the poor with a longing for bread and hope in the teeming metropolises of New Delhi, São Paulo, and Kinshasa.

And yet, Pope Benedict XVI speaks with an optimism of a new springtime for the Church. Such confidence is rooted in his trust in the Holy Spirit, the same guiding Spirit who first called him to the priesthood and then asked him to accept the Ring of the Fisherman. As he exclaimed to the jubilant throng assembled in St. Peter's Square on the afternoon of his election, "Let us move forward in the joy of the Risen Lord, confident of his unfailing help!"

Epilogue

———✠———

In man there is an inextinguishable yearning for the infinite. None of the answers attempted are sufficient. Only the God himself who became finite in order to open our finiteness and lead us to the breadth of his infiniteness responds to the question of our being. For this reason, the Christian faith finds man today too. Our task is to serve the faith with a humble spirit and the whole strength of our heart and understanding.

— Cardinal Joseph Ratzinger, 1996

As this book goes to print, Pope Benedict XVI has settled into the Vatican and has definitively claimed his place as the 264th Successor to St. Peter. He has done so with abiding humility, gratitude to Christ, and a quiet assurance that the enormous, crushing burdens of the papacy are not his alone to carry. As he said touchingly during his installation Mass:

> How can I do this? How will I be able to do it? All of you, my dear friends, have just invoked the entire host of saints, represented by some of the great names in the history of God's dealings with mankind. In this way, I too can say with renewed conviction: I am not alone. I do not have to carry alone what in truth I could never carry alone. All the saints of God are there to protect me, to sustain me and to carry me. And your prayers, my dear friends, your indulgence, your love, your faith and your hope accompany me.

In the days after the conclave, we learned from our new pontiff that he sincerely did not want to be elected, that he prayed for the choice of the Holy Spirit to pass to another. Once elected, however, he accepted, for the sake of Christ's Church, and took up his cross.

This book has attempted to offer a brief presentation of this new pontiff. As mentioned in the Introduction, this book does not claim to be the definitive study of his life. Such a book has yet to be written but will be a worthy project in the future. Instead, it has tried to take the reader on an exploration of Benedict XVI's life and writings and to offer glimpses into the often colossal issues facing the Church in which he has been engaged for over half a century.

Lost in the controversies, the deep theological documents and treatises, and the unfair caricatures that have been drawn of him over the decades, Benedict XVI is a man of prayer, of culture, of learning, and of deep faith. He loves the music of Mozart, the art of the Baroque age, the mountains of Bavaria and northern Italy, walks to Borgo Pio and the Vatican Gardens, and even soccer. Above all, he loves the Church.

Benedict has begun the same journey undertaken by all of the pontiffs. The history of the Church assures us that in the unbroken succession of Popes it is possible to remain in fidelity to the aspirations and the ideals of your immediate predecessor while leaving your own mark upon the papacy. Pope Leo XIII was elected in 1878 after the passing of Bl. Pope Pius IX after a reign of 32 years, the second longest in history after Peter. Intended to be a briefly reigning Pope, Leo went on to 25 superb years as Pope during which he ushered in a new era for the Church in the area of Catholic Social Doctrine through the encyclical *Rerum Novarum* (1891) and welcomed a new century.

Like John Paul II, Benedict XVI is aware acutely that he is now shepherd of over one billion Catholics. Like John Paul II, he knows as well that his pontificate is by the will of the Holy Spirit, and he is as he said on the night of his election, a worker in the vineyard. Our task is to assist him in those labors, to be true *cooperatores Veritatis*.

ACKNOWLEDGMENTS

There are many individuals to whom I owe a special debt of gratitude for their kind assistance in the preparation of this book: Margaret and Stephen Bunson, for their patience during the intense process of writing and research over the last days; Robert P. Lockwood, former President of Our Sunday Visitor, for his kind review and critique of the chapters; Msgr. Michael Servinsky; and Jill Kurtz, John Christensen, and Cathy Dee of Our Sunday Visitor.

Thanks are owed also to Darrin Malone, York Young, Becky Heaston, Woodene Koenig-Bricker, and George Foster of Our Sunday Visitor, as well as to Sherri Hoffman and John Laughlin, for all of their hard work in preparing the book for publication; my literary agent, Martha Casselman; and Greg Erlandson, President of Our Sunday Visitor, for his unfailing and inexplicable confidence that this project could be completed. Finally, I am especially grateful to Michael Dubruiel, my editor, for his patience, creativity, and hard work.

Appendix A
BOOKS BY POPE BENEDICT XVI (AVAILABLE IN ENGLISH)

————————✛————————

A New Song for the Lord. New York: Herder & Herder, 1996.

Behold the Pierced One. San Francisco: Ignatius Press, 1987.

Being Christian. Chicago: Franciscan Herald Press, 1970.

Called to Communion: Understanding The Church Today. San Francisco: Ignatius Press, 1996.

Co-Workers of the Truth. San Francisco: Ignatius Press, 1992.

The End of Time?: The Provocation of Talking About God. Matwah, NJ: Paulist Press, 2005.

Eschatology : Death and Eternal Life. Washington, D.C.: Catholic University of America Press, 1989.

The Feast of Faith. San Francisco: Ignatius Press, 1986.

God and the World: Believing and Living in Our Time. San Francisco: Ignatius Press, 2002.

God Is Near Us: The Eucharist, the Heart of Life. San Francisco: Ignatius Press, 2003.

Gospel, Catechesis, Catechism: Sidelights on the Catechism of the Catholic Church. San Francisco: Ignatius Press, 1997.

In the Beginning. . . : A Catholic Understanding of the Story of Creation and the Fall. Grand Rapids, MI: Wm. B. Eerdmans Publishing Company; reprint edition, 1995.

Introduction to the Catechism of the Catholic Church. San Francisco: Ignatius Press, 1994.

Introduction to Christianity. San Francisco: Ignatius Press, 2004.

Journey Towards Easter: Retreat Given in the Vatican in the Presence of Pope John Paul. New York: Crossroads, 1987.

Many Religions, One Covenant. San Francisco: Ignatius Press, 1999.

Meaning of Christian Brotherhood. San Francisco: Ignatius Press; 2nd edition, 1993.

Milestones: Memoirs: 1927 — 1977. San Francisco: Ignatius Press, 1998.

Ministers of Your Joy: Scriptural Meditations on Priestly Spirituality. Cincinnati: Servant Publications, 1989.

Nature and Mission of Theology. San Francisco: Ignatius Press 1995.

Pilgrim Fellowship of Faith: The Church as Communion. San Francisco: Ignatius Press, 2005.

Principles of Catholic Theology. San Francisco: Ignatius Press, 1987.

Principles of Christian Morality. San Francisco: Ignatius Press, 1986.

The Ratzinger Report. San Francisco: Ignatius Press, 1985.

Salt of the Earth. San Francisco: Ignatius Press; reprint edition, 1997.

Seeking God's Face. Chicago: Franciscan Herald Press, 1982.

Seek That Which is Above. San Francisco: Ignatius Press, 1986.

The Spirit of the Liturgy. San Francisco: Ignatius Press, 2000.

Theological highlights of Vatican II. Huntington, IN: Our Sunday Visitor/Matwah, NJ: Paulist Press, 1966.

Theology of History in St. Bonaventure. Chicago: Franciscan Herald Press, 1971.

To Look on Christ: Exercises in Faith, Hope, and Love. New York: Crossroad Publishing Company, 1991.

Truth and Tolerance: Christian Belief and World Religions. San Francisco: Ignatius Press, 2004.

Turning Point for Europe. San Francisco: Ignatius Press, 1994.

Appendix B

POPES OF THE ROMAN CATHOLIC CHURCH

—— ✠ ——

Information includes the name of the Pope, in many cases his name before becoming Pope, his birthplace or country of origin, the date of accession to the papacy, and the date of the end of reign that, in all but a few cases, was the date of death. Double dates indicate date of election and date of solemn beginning of ministry as Pastor of the universal Church. *Source: Annuario Pontificio, Catholic Almanac.*

St. Peter (Simon Bar-Jona): Bethsaida in Galilee; d. c. 64 or 67.

St. Linus: Tuscany; 67-76.

St. Anacletus: Rome; 76-88.

St. Clement: Rome; 88-97.

St. Evaristus: Greece; 97-105.

St. Alexander I: Rome; 105-115.

St. Sixtus I: Rome; 115-125.

St. Telesphorus: Greece; 125-136.

St. Hyginus: Greece; 136-140.

St. Pius I: Aquileia; 140-155.

St. Anicetus: Syria; 155-166.

St. Soter: Campania; 166-175.

St. Eleutherius: Nicopolis in Epirus; 175-189.

St. Victor I: Africa; 189-199.

St. Zephyrinus: Rome; 199-217.

St. Callistus I: Rome; 217-222.

St. Urban I: Rome; 222-230.

St. Pontian: Rome; July 21, 230, to Sept. 28, 235.

St. Anterus: Greece; Nov. 21, 235, to Jan. 3, 236.

St. Fabian: Rome; Jan. 10, 236, to Jan. 20, 250.

St. Cornelius: Rome; Mar. 251 to June 253.

St. Lucius I: Rome; June 25, 253, to Mar. 5, 254.

St. Stephen I: Rome; May 12, 254, to Aug. 2, 257.

St. Sixtus II: Greece; Aug. 30, 257, to Aug. 6, 258.

St. Dionysius: birthplace unknown; July 22, 259, to Dec. 26, 268.

St. Felix I: Rome; Jan. 5, 269, to Dec. 30, 274.

St. Eutychian: Luni; Jan. 4, 275, to Dec. 7, 283.

St. Caius: Dalmatia; Dec. 17, 283, to Apr. 22, 296.

St. Marcellinus: Rome; June 30, 296, to Oct. 25, 304.

St. Marcellus I: Rome; May 27, 308, or June 26, 308, to Jan. 16, 309.

St. Eusebius: Greece; Apr. 18, 309, to Aug. 17, 309 or 310.

St. Melchiades (Miltiades): Africa; July 2, 311, to Jan. 11, 314.

St. Sylvester I: Rome; Jan. 31, 314, to Dec. 31, 335.

St. Marcus: Rome; Jan. 18, 336, to Oct. 7, 336.

St. Julius I: Rome; Feb. 6, 337, to Apr. 12, 352.

Liberius: Rome; May 17, 352, to Sept. 24, 366.

St. Damasus I: Spain; Oct. 1, 366, to Dec. 11, 384.

St. Siricius: Rome; Dec. 15, or 22 or 29, 384, to Nov. 26, 399.

St. Anastasius I: Rome; Nov. 27, 399, to Dec. 19, 401.

St. Innocent I: Albano; Dec. 22, 401, to Mar. 12, 417.

St. Zosimus: Greece; Mar. 18, 417, to Dec. 26, 418.

St. Boniface I: Rome; Dec. 28 or 29, 418, to Sept. 4, 422.

St. Celestine I: Campania; Sept. 10, 422, to July 27, 432.

St. Sixtus III: Rome; July 31, 432, to Aug. 19, 440.

St. Leo I the Great: Tuscany; Sept. 29, 440, to Nov. 10, 461.

St. Hilary: Sardinia; Nov. 19, 461, to Feb. 29, 468.

St. Simplicius: Tivoli; Mar. 3, 468, to Mar. 10, 483.

St. Felix III (II): Rome; Mar. 13, 483, to Mar. 1, 492.

St. Gelasius I: Africa; Mar. 1, 492, to Nov. 21, 496.

Anastasius II: Rome; Nov. 24, 496, to Nov. 19, 498.

St. Symmachus: Sardinia; Nov. 22, 498, to July 19, 514.

St. Hormisdas: Frosinone; July 20, 514, to Aug. 6, 523.

St. John I: Tuscany; Aug. 13, 523, to May 18, 526.

St. Felix IV (III): Samnium; July 12, 526, to Sept. 22, 530.

Boniface II: Rome; Sept. 22, 530, to Oct. 17, 532.

John II: Rome; Jan. 2, 533, to May 8, 535.

St. Agapitus I: Rome; May 13, 535, to Apr. 22, 536.

St. Silverius: Campania; June 1 or 8, 536, to Nov. 11, 537 (d. Dec. 2, 537).

Vigilius: Rome; Mar. 29, 537, to June 7, 555.

Pelagius I: Rome; Apr. 16, 556, to Mar. 4, 561.

John III: Rome; July 17, 561, to July 13, 574.

Benedict I: Rome; June 2, 575, to July 30, 579.

Pelagius II: Rome; Nov. 26, 579, to Feb. 7, 590.

St. Gregory I the Great: Rome; Sept. 3, 590, to Mar. 12, 604.

Sabinian: Blera in Tuscany; Sept. 13, 604, to Feb. 22, 606.

Boniface III: Rome; Feb. 19, 607, to Nov. 12, 607.

St. Boniface IV: Abruzzi; Aug. 25, 608, to May 8, 615.

St. Deusdedit (Adeodatus I): Rome; Oct. 19, 615, to Nov. 8, 618.

Boniface V: Naples; Dec. 23, 619, to Oct. 25, 625.

Honorius I: Campania; Oct. 27, 625, to Oct. 12, 638.

Severinus: Rome; May 28, 640, to Aug. 2, 640.

John IV: Dalmatia; Dec. 24, 640, to Oct. 12, 642.

Theodore I: Greece; Nov. 24, 642, to May 14, 649.

St. Martin I: Todi; July, 649, to Sept. 16, 655 (in exile from June 17, 653).

St. Eugene I: Rome; Aug. 10, 654, to June 2, 657.

St. Vitalian: Segni; July 30, 657, to Jan. 27, 672.

Adeodatus II: Rome; Apr. 11, 672, to June 17, 676.

Donus: Rome; Nov. 2, 676, to Apr. 11, 678.

St. Agatho: Sicily; June 27, 678, to Jan. 10, 681.

St. Leo II: Sicily; Aug. 17, 682, to July 3, 683.

St. Benedict II: Rome; June 26, 684, to May 8, 685.

John V: Syria; July 23, 685, to Aug. 2, 686.

Conon: birthplace unknown; Oct. 21, 686, to Sept. 21, 687.

St. Sergius I: Syria; Dec. 15, 687, to Sept. 8, 701.

John VI: Greece; Oct. 30, 701, to Jan. 11, 705.

John VII: Greece; Mar. 1, 705, to Oct. 18, 707.

Sisinnius: Syria; Jan. 15, 708, to Feb. 4, 708.

Constantine: Syria; Mar. 25, 708, to Apr. 9, 715.

St. Gregory II: Rome; May 19, 715, to Feb. 11, 731.

St. Gregory III: Syria; Mar. 18, 731, to Nov. 741.

St. Zachary: Greece; Dec. 10, 741, to Mar. 22, 752.

Stephen II (III): Rome; Mar. 26, 752, to Apr. 26, 757.

St. Paul I: Rome; Apr. (May 29), 757, to June 28, 767.

Stephen III (IV): Sicily; Aug. 1 (7), 768, to Jan. 24, 772.

Adrian I: Rome; Feb. 1 (9), 772, to Dec. 25, 795.

St. Leo III: Rome; Dec. 26 (27), 795, to June 12, 816.

Stephen IV (V): Rome; June 22, 816, to Jan. 24, 817.

St. Paschal I: Rome; Jan. 25, 817, to Feb. 11, 824.

Eugene II: Rome; Feb. (May) 824 to Aug. 827.

Valentine: Rome; Aug. 827, to Sept. 827.

Gregory IV: Rome; 827, to Jan. 844.

Sergius II: Rome; Jan. 844 to Jan. 27, 847.

St. Leo IV: Rome; Jan. (Apr. 10) 847, to July 17, 855.

Benedict III: Rome; July (Sept. 29), 855, to Apr. 17, 858.

St. Nicholas I the Great: Rome; Apr. 24, 858, to Nov. 13, 867.

Adrian II: Rome; Dec. 14, 867, to Dec. 14, 872.

John VIII: Rome; Dec. 14, 872, to Dec. 16, 882.

Marinus I: Gallese; Dec. 16, 882, to May 15, 884.

St. Adrian III: Rome; May 17, 884, to Sept. 885. Cult confirmed June 2, 1891.

Stephen V (VI): Rome; Sept. 885, to Sept. 14, 891.

Formosus: Bishop of Porto; Oct. 6, 891, to Apr. 4, 896.

Boniface VI: Rome; Apr. 896 to Apr. 896.

Stephen VI (VII): Rome; May 896 to Aug. 897.

Romanus: Gallese; Aug. 897 to Nov. 897.

Theodore II: Rome; Dec. 897 to Dec. 897.

John IX: Tivoli; Jan. 898 to Jan. 900.

Benedict IV: Rome; Jan. (Feb.) 900 to July 903.

Leo V: Ardea; July 903 to Sept. 903.

Sergius III: Rome; Jan. 29, 904, to Apr. 14, 911.

Anastasius III: Rome; Apr. 911 to June 913.

Landus: Sabina; July 913 to Feb. 914.

John X: Tossignano (Imola); Mar. 914 to May 928.

Leo VI: Rome; May 928 to Dec. 928.

Stephen VII (VIII): Rome; Dec. 928 to Feb. 931.

John XI: Rome; Feb. (Mar.) 931 to Dec. 935.

Leo VII: Rome; Jan. 3, 936, to July 13, 939.

Stephen VIII (IX): Rome; July 14, 939, to Oct. 942.

Marinus II: Rome; Oct. 30, 942, to May 946.

Agapitus II: Rome; May 10, 946, to Dec. 955.

John XII (Octavius): Tusculum; Dec. 16, 955, to May 14, 964 (date of his death).

Leo VIII: Rome; Dec. 4 (6), 963, to Mar. 1, 965.

Benedict V: Rome; May 22, 964, to July 4, 966.

John XIII: Rome; Oct. 1, 965, to Sept. 6, 972.

Benedict VI: Rome; Jan. 19, 973 to June 974.

Benedict VII: Rome; Oct. 974 to July 10, 983.

John XIV (Peter Campenora): Pavia; Dec., 983 to Aug. 20, 984.

John XV: Rome; Aug. 985 to Mar. 996.

Gregory V (Bruno of Carinthia): Saxony; May 3, 996, to Feb. 18, 999.

Sylvester II (Gerbert): Auvergne; Apr. 2, 999, to May 12, 1003.

John XVII (Siccone): Rome; June 1003 to Dec. 1003.

John XVIII (Phasianus): Rome; Jan. 1004, to July 1009.

Sergius IV (Peter): Rome; July 31, 1009, to May 12, 1012.

Benedict VIII (Theophylactus): Tusculum; May 18, 1012, to Apr. 9, 1024.

John XIX (Romanus): Tusculum; Apr. (May) 1024 to 1032.

Benedict IX (Theophylactus): Tusculum; 1032 to 1044.

Sylvester III (John): Rome; Jan. 20, 1045, to Feb. 10, 1045.

Benedict IX (second time): Apr. 10, 1045, to May 1, 1045.

Gregory VI (John Gratian): Rome; May 5, 1045, to Dec. 20, 1046.

Clement II (Suitger, Lord of Morsleben and Hornburg): Saxony; Dec. 24 (25), 1046 to Oct. 9, 1047.

Benedict IX (third time): Nov. 8, 1047, to July 17, 1048 (d. c. 1055).

Damasus II (Poppo): Bavaria; July 17, 1048, to Aug. 9, 1048.

St. Leo IX (Bruno): Alsace; Feb. 12, 1049, to Apr. 19, 1054.

Victor II (Gebhard): Swabia; Apr. 16, 1055, to July 28, 1057.

Stephen IX (X) (Frederick): Lorraine; Aug. 3, 1057, to Mar. 29, 1058.

Nicholas II (Gerard): Burgundy; Jan. 24, 1059, to July 27, 1061.

Alexander II (Anselmo da Baggio): Milan; Oct. 1, 1061, to Apr. 21, 1073.

St. Gregory VII (Hildebrand): Tuscany; Apr. 22 (June 30), 1073, to May 25, 1085.

Bl. Victor III (Dauferius; Desiderius): Benevento; May 24, 1086, to Sept. 16, 1087.

Bl. Urban II (Otto di Lagery): France; Mar. 12, 1088, to July 29, 1099.

Paschal II (Raniero): Ravenna; Aug. 13 (14), 1099, to Jan. 21, 1118.

Gelasius II (Giovanni Caetani): Gaeta; Jan. 24 (Mar. 10), 1118, to Jan. 28, 1119.

Callistus II (Guido of Burgundy): Burgundy; Feb. 2 (9), 1119, to Dec. 13, 1124.

Honorius II (Lamberto): Fiagnano (Imola); Dec. 15 (21), 1124, to Feb. 13, 1130.

Innocent II (Gregorio Papareschi): Rome; Feb. 14 (23), 1130, to Sept. 24, 1143.

Celestine II (Guido): Citta di Castello; Sept. 26 (Oct. 3), 1143, to Mar. 8, 1144.

Lucius II (Gerardo Caccianemici): Bologna: Mar. 12, 1144, to Feb. 15, 1145.

Bl. Eugene III (Bernardo Paganelli di Montemagno): Pisa; Feb. 15 (18), 1145, to July 8, 1153.

Anastasius IV (Corrado): Rome; July 12, 1153, to Dec, 3, 1154.

Adrian IV (Nicholas Breakspear): England; Dec. 4 (5), 1154, to Sept. 1, 1159.

Alexander III (Rolando Bandinelli): Siena; Sept. 7 (20), 1159, to Aug. 30, 1181.

Lucius III (Ubaldo Allucingoli): Lucca; Sept. 1 (6), 1181, to Sept. 25, 1185.

Urban III (Uberto Crivelli): Milan; Nov. 25 (Dec. 1), 1185, to Oct. 20, 1187.

Gregory VIII (Alberto de Morra): Benevento; Oct. 21 (25), 1187, to Dec. 17, 1187.

Clement III (Paolo Scolari): Rome; Dec. 19 (20), 1187, to Mar. 1191.

Celestine III (Giacinto Bobone): Rome; Mar. 30 (Apr. 14), 1191, to Jan. 8, 1198.

Innocent III (Lotario dei Conti di Segni); Anagni; Jan. 8 (Feb. 22), 1198, to July 16, 1216.

Honorius III (Cencio Savelli): Rome; July 18 (24), 1216, to Mar. 18, 1227.

Gregory IX (Ugolino, Count of Segni): Anagni; Mar. 19 (21), 1227, to Aug. 22, 1241.

Celestine IV (Goffredo Castiglioni): Milan; Oct. 25 (28), 1241, to Nov. 10, 1241.

Innocent IV (Sinibaldo Fieschi): Genoa; June 25 (28), 1243, to Dec. 7, 1254.

Alexander IV (Rinaldo, House of Ienne): Ienne (Rome); Dec. 12 (20), 1254, to May 25, 1261.

Urban IV (Jacques Pantaléon): Troyes; Aug. 29 (Sept. 4), 1261, to Oct. 2, 1264.

Clement IV (Guy Foulques or Guido le Gros): France; Feb. 5 (15), 1265, to Nov. 29, 1268.

Bl. Gregory X (Teobaldo Visconti): Piacenza; Sept. 1, 1271 (Mar. 27, 1272), to Jan. 10, 1276.

Bl. Innocent V (Peter of Tarentaise): Savoy; Jan. 21 (Feb. 22), 1276, to June 22, 1276.

Adrian V (Ottobono Fieschi): Genoa: July 11, 1276, to Aug. 18, 1276.

John XXI (Petrus Juliani or Petrus Hispanus): Portugal; Sept. 8 (20), 1276, to May 20, 1277.

Nicholas III (Giovanni Gaetano Orsini): Rome; Nov. 25 (Dec. 26), 1277, to Aug. 22, 1280.

Martin IV (Simon de Brie): France; Feb. 22 (Mar. 23), 1281, to Mar. 28, 1285.

Honorius IV (Giacomo Savelli): Rome; Apr. 2 (May 20), 1285, to Apr. 3, 1287.

Nicholas IV (Girolamo Masci): Ascoli; Feb. 22, 1288, to Apr. 4, 1292.

St. Celestine V (Pietro del Murrone): Isernia; July 5 (Aug. 29), 1294, to Dec. 13, 1294; d. May 19, 1296.

Boniface VIII (Benedetto Caetani): Anagni; Dec. 24, 1294 (Jan. 23, 1295), to Oct. 11, 1303.

Bl. Benedict XI (Niccolo Boccasini): Treviso; Oct. 22 (27), 1303, to July 7, 1304.

Clement V (Bertrand de Got): France; June 5 (Nov. 14), 1305, to Apr. 20, 1314.

John XXII (Jacques d'Euse): Cahors; Aug. 7 (Sept. 5), 1316, to Dec. 4, 1334.

Benedict XII (Jacques Fournier): France; Dec. 20, 1334 (Jan. 8, 1335), to Apr. 25, 1342.

Clement VI (Pierre Roger): France; May 7 (19), 1342, to Dec. 6, 1352.

Innocent VI (Etienne Aubert): France; Dec. 18 (30), 1352, to Sept. 12, 1362.

Bl. Urban V (Guillaume de Grimoard): France; Sept. 28 (Nov. 6), 1362, to Dec. 19, 1370.

Gregory XI (Pierre Roger de Beaufort): France; Dec. 30, 1370 (Jan. 5, 1371), to Mar. 26, 1378.

Urban VI (Bartolomeo Prignano): Naples; Apr. 8 (18), 1378, to Oct. 15, 1389.

Boniface IX (Pietro Tomacelli): Naples; Nov. 2 (9), 1389, to Oct. 1, 1404.

Innocent VII (Cosma Migliorati): Sulmona; Oct. 17 (Nov. 11), 1404, to Nov. 6, 1406.

Gregory XII (Angelo Correr): Venice; Nov. 30 (Dec. 19), 1406, to July 4, 1415, when he voluntarily resigned from the papacy to permit the election of his successor. He died Oct. 18, 1417.

Martin V (Oddone Colonna): Rome; Nov. 11 (21), 1417, to Feb. 20, 1431.

Eugene IV (Gabriele Condulmer): Venice; Mar. 3 (11), 1431, to Feb. 23, 1447.

Nicholas V (Tommaso Parentucelli): Sarzana; Mar. 6 (19), 1447, to Mar. 24, 1455.

Callistus III (Alfonso Borgia): Jativa (Valencia); Apr. 8 (20), 1455, to Aug. 6, 1458.

Pius II (Enea Silvio Piccolomini): Siena; Aug. 19 (Sept. 3), 1458, to Aug. 14, 1464.

Paul II (Pietro Barbo): Venice; Aug. 30 (Sept. 16), 1464, to July 26, 1471.

Sixtus IV (Francesco della Rovere): Savona; Aug. 9 (25), 1471, to Aug. 12, 1484.

Innocent VIII (Giovanni Battista Cibo): Genoa; Aug. 29 (Sept. 12), 1484, to July 25, 1492.

Alexander VI (Rodrigo Borgia): Jativa (Valencia); Aug. 11 (26), 1492, to Aug. 18, 1503.

Pius III (Francesco Todeschini-Piccolomini): Siena; Sept. 22 (Oct. 1, 8), 1503, to Oct. 18, 1503.

Julius II (Giuliano della Rovere): Savona; Oct. 31 (Nov. 26), 1503, to Feb. 21, 1513.

Leo X (Giovanni de' Medici): Florence; Mar. 9 (19), 1513, to Dec. 1, 1521.

Adrian VI (Adrian Florensz): Utrecht; Jan. 9 (Aug. 31), 1522, to Sept. 14, 1523.

Clement VII (Giulio de' Medici): Florence; Nov. 19 (26), 1523, to Sept. 25, 1534.

Paul III (Alessandro Farnese): Rome; Oct. 13 (Nov. 3), 1534, to Nov. 10, 1549.

Julius III (Giovanni Maria Ciocchi del Monte): Rome; Feb. 7 (22), 1550, to Mar. 23, 1555.

Marcellus II (Marcello Cervini): Montepulciano; Apr. 9 (10), 1555, to May 1, 1555.

Paul IV (Gian Pietro Carafa): Naples; May 23 (26), 1555, to Aug. 18, 1559.

Pius IV (Giovan Angelo de' Medici): Milan; Dec. 25, 1559 (Jan. 6, 1560), to Dec. 9, 1565.

St. Pius V (Antonio-Michele Ghislieri): Bosco (Alexandria); Jan. 7 (17), 1566, to May 1, 1572.

Gregory XIII (Ugo Buoncompagni): Bologna; May 13 (25), 1572, to Apr. 10, 1585.

Sixtus V (Felice Peretti): Grottammare (Ripatransone); Apr. 24 (May 1), 1585, to Aug. 27, 1590.

Urban VII (Giambattista Castagna): Rome; Sept. 15, 1590, to Sept. 27, 1590.

Gregory XIV (Niccolo Sfondrati): Cremona; Dec. 5 (8), 1590, to Oct. 16, 1591.

Innocent IX (Giovanni Antonio Facchinetti): Bologna; Oct. 29 (Nov. 3), 1591, to Dec. 30, 1591.

Clement VIII (Ippolito Aldobrandini): Florence; Jan. 30 (Feb. 9), 1592, to Mar. 3, 1605.

Leo XI (Alessandro de' Medici): Florence; Apr. 1 (10), 1605, to Apr. 27, 1605.

Paul V (Camillo Borghese): Rome; May 16 (29), 1605, to Jan. 28, 1621.

Gregory XV (Alessandro Ludovisi): Bologna; Feb. 9 (14), 1621, to July 8, 1623.

Urban VIII (Maffeo Barberini): Florence; Aug. 6 (Sept. 29), 1623, to July 29, 1644.

Innocent X (Giovanni Battista Pamfili): Rome; Sept. 15 (Oct. 4), 1644, to Jan. 7, 1655.

Alexander VII (Fabio Chigi): Siena; Apr. 7 (18), 1655, to May 22, 1667.

Clement IX (Giulio Rospigliosi): Pistoia; June 20 (26), 1667, to Dec. 9, 1669.

Clement X (Emilio Altieri): Rome; Apr. 29 (May 11), 1670, to July 22, 1676.

Bl. Innocent XI (Benedetto Odescalchi): Como; Sept. 21 (Oct. 4), 1676, to Aug. 12, 1689.

Alexander VIII (Pietro Ottoboni): Venice; Oct. 6 (16), 1689, to Feb. 1, 1691.

Innocent XII (Antonio Pignatelli): Spinazzola (Venosa); July 12 (15), 1691, to Sept. 27, 1700.

Clement XI (Giovanni Francesco Albani): Urbino; Nov. 23, 30 (Dec. 8), 1700, to Mar. 19, 1721.

Innocent XIII (Michelangelo dei Conti): Rome; May 8 (18), 1721, to Mar. 7, 1724.

Benedict XIII (Pietro Francesco Vincenzo Maria Orsini): Gravina (Bari); May 29 (June 4), 1724, to Feb. 21, 1730.

Clement XII (Lorenzo Corsini): Florence; July 12 (16), 1730, to Feb. 6, 1740.

Benedict XIV (Prospero Lambertini): Bologna; Aug. 17 (22), 1740, to May 3, 1758.

Clement XIII (Carlo Rezzonico): Venice; July 6 (16), 1758, to Feb. 2, 1769.

Clement XIV (Giovanni Vincenzo Antonio Lorenzo Ganganelli): Rimini; May 19, 28 (June 4), 1769, to Sept. 22, 1774.

Pius VI (Giovanni Angelo Braschi): Cesena; Feb. 15 (22), 1775, to Aug. 29, 1799.

Pius VII (Barnaba Gregorio Chiaramonti): Cesena; Mar. 14 (21), 1800, to Aug. 20, 1823.

Leo XII (Annibale della Genga): Genga (Fabriano); Sept. 28 (Oct. 5), 1823, to Feb. 10, 1829.

Pius VIII (Francesco Saverio Castiglioni): Cingoli; Mar. 31 (Apr. 5), 1829, to Nov. 30, 1830.

Gregory XVI (Bartolomeo Alberto-Mauro-Cappellari): Belluno; Feb. 2 (6), 1831, to June 1, 1846.

Bl. Pius IX (Giovanni M. Mastai-Ferretti): Senigallia; June 16 (21), 1846, to Feb. 7, 1878.

Leo XIII (Gioacchino Pecci): Carpineto (Anagni); Feb. 20 (Mar. 3), 1878, to July 20, 1903.

St. Pius X (Giuseppe Sarto): Riese (Treviso); Aug. 4 (9), 1903, to Aug. 20, 1914. Canonized May 29, 1954.

Benedict XV (Giacomo della Chiesa): Genoa; Sept. 3 (6), 1914, to Jan. 22, 1922.

Pius XI (Achille Ratti): Desio (Milan); Feb. 6 (12), 1922, to Feb. 10, 1939.

Pius XII (Eugenio Pacelli): Rome; Mar. 2 (12), 1939, to Oct. 9, 1958.

Bl. John XXIII (Angelo Giuseppe Roncalli): Sotto il Monte (Bergamo); Oct. 28 (Nov. 4), 1958, to June 3, 1963.

Paul VI (Giovanni Battista Montini): Concessio (Brescia); June 21 (30), 1963, to Aug. 6, 1978.

John Paul I (Albino Luciani): Forno di Canale (Belluno); Aug. 26 (Sept. 3), 1978, to Sept. 28, 1978.

John Paul II (Karol Wojtyla): Wadowice, Poland; Oct. 16 (22), 1978, to April 2, 2005.

Benedict XVI (Joseph Ratzinger): Marktl am Inn, Germany; April 19 (24), 2005 to Present.

GLOSSARY

———— ✠ ————

Aggiornamento: An Italian word having the general meaning of bringing up to date, renewal, revitalization, descriptive of the processes of spiritual renewal and institutional reform and change in the Church; fostered by the Second Vatican Council.

Apostolic Succession: Bishops of the Church, who form a collective body or college, are successors to the Apostles by ordination and divine right; as such they carry on the mission entrusted by Christ to the Apostles as guardians and teachers of the deposit of faith, principal pastors and spiritual authorities of the faithful. The doctrine of apostolic succession is based on New Testament evidence and the constant teaching of the Church, reflected as early as the end of the 1st century in a letter of Pope St. Clement to the Corinthians. A significant facet of the doctrine is the role of the Pope as the successor of St. Peter, the vicar of Christ and head of the college of bishops. The doctrine of apostolic succession means more than continuity of apostolic faith and doctrine; its basic requisite is ordination by the laying on of hands in apostolic succession.

Authority, Ecclesiastical: The authority exercised by the Church, and particularly by the Pope and the bishops; it is delegated by Jesus Christ to St. Peter. This authority extends to all those matters entrusted to the Apostles by Christ, including teaching of the Faith, the liturgy and sacraments, moral guidance, and the administration of discipline.

Baldacchino: A canopy over an altar.

Biglietto: A papal document of notification of appointment to the cardinalate.

Blessing: Invocation of God's favor, by official ministers of the Church or by private individuals. Blessings are recounted in the Old and New Testaments, and are common in the Christian tradition. Many types of blessings are listed in the Book of Blessings of the Roman Ritual. Private blessings, as well as those of an official kind, are efficacious. Blessings are imparted with the Sign of the Cross and appropriate prayer.

Brief, Apostolic: A papal letter, less formal than a bull, signed for the Pope by a secretary and impressed with the seal of the Fisherman's Ring. Simple apostolic letters of this kind are issued for beatifications and with respect to other matters.

Bull, Apostolic: Apostolic letter, a solemn form of papal document, beginning with the name and title of the Pope (e.g., John Paul II, Servant of the Servants of God), dealing with an important subject, sealed with a *bulla* or red-ink imprint of the device on the *bulla*. Bulls are issued to confer the titles of Bishops and Cardinals, to promulgate canonizations, to proclaim Holy Years and for other purposes. A collection of bulls is called a *bullarium*.

Camerlengo (**Chamberlain**): (1) the Chamberlain of the Holy Roman Church is a Cardinal with special responsibilities, especially during the time between the death of one Pope and the election of his successor; among other things, he safeguards and administers the goods and revenues of the Holy See and heads particular congregations of Cardinals for special purposes. The current Camerlengo is Cardinal Eduardo Martinez Somalo. (2) the Chamberlain of the College of Cardinals has charge of the property and revenues of the College and keeps the record of business transacted in consistories. (3) the Chamberlain of the Roman Clergy is the president of the secular clergy of Rome.

Canon Law: The Code of Canon Law (*Corpus Iuris Canonici*) enacted and promulgated by ecclesiastical authority for the orderly and pastoral administration and government of the Church. A revised Code for the Latin Rite, effective Nov. 27, 1983, consists of 1,752 canons in seven books under the titles of general norms, the people of God, the teaching mission of the Church, the sanctifying mission of the Church, temporal goods of the Church, penal law and procedural law. The antecedent of this Code was promulgated in 1917 and became effective in 1918; it consisted of 2,414 canons in five books covering general rules, ecclesiastical persons, sacred things, trials, crimes and punishments. There is a separate Code of the Canons of Eastern Churches, in effect since Oct. 1, 1991.

Cardinal: Member of the Sacred College of Cardinals and a high-ranking, powerful member of the Church hierarchy. He gives assistance to the Pope in the government of the Church and has the important task of taking part in the election of a new successor of St. Peter. By canon law, all Cardinals must be ordained priests; those who are not bishops at the time of their elevation are consecrated to the episcopacy.

Catechism: A systematic presentation of the fundamentals of Catholic doctrine regarding faith and morals. Sources are Sacred Scripture, tradition, the magisterium (teaching authority of the Church), the writings of Fathers and Doctors of the Church, liturgy. The new *Catechism of the Catholic Church*, published Oct. 11, 1992, consists of four principal sections: the profession of faith, (the Creed), the sacraments of faith, the life of faith (the Commandments) and the prayer of the believer (the Lord's Prayer). The 16th century Council of Trent mandated publication of the *Roman Catechism*. Catechisms such as these two are useful sources for other catechisms serving particular needs of the faithful and persons seeking admission to the Catholic Church.

Cathedra: A Greek word for chair, designating the chair or seat of a bishop in the principal church of his diocese, which is therefore called a cathedral.

Catholic: A Greek word, meaning universal, first used in the title Catholic Church in a letter written by St. Ignatius of Antioch about 107 to the Christians of Smyrna.

Ceremonies, Master of: One who directs the proceedings of a rite or ceremony during that function. The Papal Master of Ceremonies has responsibility for organizing all papal liturgies. The current Papal Master of Ceremonies is Archbishop Piero Marini.

Chirograph or Autograph Letter: A letter written by a Pope himself, in his own handwriting.

Christology: Branch of theology concerned with the person and nature of Jesus Christ, with particular attention paid to his Divine Person and his two natures, human and divine. It should not be confused with soteriology, the branch of theology concerned with Christ's labors of salvation.

Clergy: Men ordained to holy orders and commissioned for sacred ministries and assigned to pastoral and other duties for the service of the people and the Church: (1) Diocesan or secular clergy are committed to pastoral ministry in parishes and in other capacities in a particular church (diocese) under the direction of their bishop, to whom they are bound by a promise of obedience. (2) Regular clergy belong to religious institutes (orders, congregations, societies — institutes of consecrated life) and are so called because they observe the rule (*regula*, in Latin) of their respective institutes. They are committed to the ways of life and apostolates of their institutes. In ordinary pastoral ministry, they are under the direction of local bishops as well as their own superiors.

Collegiality: A term in use especially since the Second Vatican Council to describe the authority exercised by the College of Bishops. The bishops of the Church, in union with and subordinate to the Pope — who has full, supreme and universal power over the Church which he can always exercise independently — have supreme teaching and pastoral authority over the whole Church. In addition to their proper authority of office for the good of the faithful in their respective dioceses or other jurisdictions, the bishops have authority to act for the good of the universal Church. This collegial authority is exercised in a solemn manner in an ecumenical council and can also be exercised in other ways sanctioned by the Pope. Doctrine on collegiality was set forth by the Second Vatican Council in *Lumen Gentium* (the Dogmatic Constitution on the Church). (See separate entry.) By extension, the concept of collegiality is applied to other forms of participation and co-responsibility by members of a community.

Conclave: The term used for the formal gathering of the members of the College of Cardinals to elect a new Pope. The name, taken from the Latin, *cum clavis* ("with a key"), is derived from the fact that since 1274 the Cardinals are sequestered until they reach a decision on the new successor to St. Peter. Only Cardinals under the age of 80 are eligible to participate. Starting with the conclave of 1878, every such gathering has been held in the Sistine Chapel.

Concordat: A church-state treaty with the force of law concerning matters of mutual concern — e.g., rights of the Church, arrangement of ecclesiastical jurisdictions, marriage laws, education. Approximately 150 agreements of this kind have been negotiated since the Concordat of Worms in 1122.

Congregation: (1) The collective name for the people who form a parish. (2) One of the chief administrative departments of the Roman Curia. (3) An unofficial term for a group of men and women who belong to a religious community or institute of consecrated life.

Consistory: An assembly of Cardinals presided over by the Pope.

Constitution: (1) An apostolic or papal constitution is a document in which a Pope enacts and promulgates law. (2) A formal and solemn document issued by an ecumenical council on a doctrinal or pastoral subject, with binding force in the whole Church; e.g., the four constitutions issued by the Second Vatican Council on the Church, liturgy, revelation, and the Church in the modern world. (3) The constitutions of institutes of consecrated life and societies of apostolic life spell out details of and norms drawn from the various rules for the guidance and direction of the life and work of their members.

Council: A formal meeting of Church leaders, summoned by a bishop or appropriate Church leader, with the general purpose of assisting the life of the Church through deliberations, decrees, and promulgations. Different councils include: diocesan councils (synod), a gathering of the officials of an individual diocese; provincial councils, the meeting of the bishops of a province; plenary councils, the assembly of the bishops of a country; and ecumenical councils, a gathering of all the bishops in the world under the authority of the Bishop of Rome.

Crosier: The bishop's staff, symbolic of his pastoral office, responsibility and authority; used at liturgical functions.

Crypt: An underground or partly underground chamber; e.g., the lower part of a church used for worship and/or burial.

Cura Animarum: A Latin phrase, meaning care of souls, designating the pastoral ministry and responsibility of bishops and priests.

Curia: The personnel and offices through which (1) the Pope administers the affairs of the universal Church, the Roman Curia, or (2) a bishop the affairs of a diocese, diocesan curia. The principal officials of a diocesan curia are the vicar general of the diocese, the chancellor, officials of the diocesan tribunal or court, examiners, consultors, auditors, notaries.

Dean: (1) A priest with supervisory responsibility over a section of a diocese known as a deanery. The post-Vatican II counterpart of a dean is an episcopal vicar. (2) The senior or ranking member of a group.

Declaration: (1) An ecclesiastical document which presents an interpretation of an existing law. (2) A position paper on a specific subject; e.g., the three declarations issued by the Second Vatican Council on religious freedom, non-Christian religions, and Christian education.

Decree: An edict or ordinance issued by a Pope and/or by an ecumenical council, with binding force in the whole Church; by a department of the Roman Curia, with binding force for concerned parties; by a territorial body of bishops, with binding force for persons in the area; by individual bishops, with binding force for concerned parties until revocation or the death of the bishop. The nine decrees issued by the Second Vatican Council were combinations of doctrinal and pastoral statements with executive orders for action and movement toward renewal and reform in the Church.

Deposit of the Faith: The body of saving truth, entrusted by Christ to the Apostles and handed on by them to the Church to be preserved and proclaimed. As embodied in Revelation and Tradition the term is very nearly coextensive with objective revelation, in that it embraces the whole of Christ's teaching. But the term "deposit" highlights particular features of the apostolic teaching implying that this teaching is an inexhaustible store that rewards and promotes reflection and study so that new insights and deeper penetration might be made into the mystery of the divine economy of salvation. Although our understanding of this teaching can develop, it can never be augmented in its substance; the teaching is a divine trust, which cannot be altered, modified, or debased. The term *depositum fidei* first entered official Catholic teaching with the Council of Trent, but its substance is well-attested in the Scriptures and the Fathers.

Dicastery: A broad term used for the various offices and departments of the Roman Curia,

Diocese: A particular church, a fully organized ecclesiastical jurisdiction under the pastoral direction of a bishop as local Ordinary.

Ecclesiology: Study of the nature, constitution, members, mission, functions, etc., of the Church.

Ecumenism: The movement of Christians and their churches toward the unity willed by Christ. The Second Vatican Council called the movement "those activities and enterprises which, according to various needs of the Church and opportune occasions, are started and organized for the fostering of unity among Christians" (Decree on Ecumenism, No. 4). Spiritual ecumenism, i.e., mutual prayer for unity, is the heart of the movement. The movement also involves scholarly and pew-level efforts for the development of mutual understanding and better interfaith relations in general, and collaboration by the churches and their members in the social area.

Encyclical: The highest form of papal teaching document. It is normally addressed to all the bishops and/or to all the faithful.

Episcopate: (1) The office, dignity and sacramental powers bestowed upon a bishop at his ordination. (2) The body of bishops collectively.

Ethics: Moral philosophy, the science of the morality of human acts deriving from natural law, the natural end of man, and the powers of human reason. It includes all the spheres of human activity — personal, social, economic, political, etc. Ethics is distinct from but can be related to moral theology, whose primary principles are drawn from divine revelation.

Evangelization: Proclamation of the Gospel, the Good News of salvation in and through Christ, among those who have not yet known or received it; and efforts for the progressive development of the life of faith among those who have already received the Gospel and all that it entails. Evangelization is the primary mission of the Church, in which all members of the Church are called to participate.

Excommunication: A penalty or censure by which a baptized Roman Catholic is excluded from the communion of the faithful, for committing and remaining obstinate in certain serious offenses specified in canon law: e.g., heresy, schism, apostasy, abortion. As by baptism a person is made a member of the Church in which there is a communication of spiritual goods, so by excommunication he is deprived of the same spiritual goods until he repents and receives absolution. Even though excommunicated, a person is still responsible for fulfillment of the normal obligations of a Catholic.

Fisherman's Ring: A signet ring (termed in Italian the *pescatorio*) engraved with the image of St. Peter fishing from a boat, and encircled with the name of the reigning Pope. It is not worn by the Pope. It is used to seal briefs, and is destroyed after each Pope's death.

General Congregation: The name used for the meetings of the Cardinals in Rome that are held during the *sede vacante*. The purpose of the meetings is limited strictly to the preparations for the funeral of the deceased Pope and the preparations for the conclave. The Cardinals are not permitted to appoint new members to the College of Cardinals or set aside any provisions of the regulations under which the activities of the *sede vacante* are governed.

Hierarchy: The authorities of order who carry out the sacramental, teaching, and pastoral ministry of the Church; the hierarchy consists of the

Pope, bishops, priests, and deacons; the Pope and the bishops give pastoral governance to the faithful.

Holy Father: A title used for the Pope; it is a shortened translation of the Latin title *Beatissimus Pater*, "Most Blessed Father" and refers to his position as the spiritual father of all the Christian faithful.

Holy See: (1) The diocese of the Pope, Rome. (2) The Pope himself and/or the various officials and bodies of the Church's central administration at Vatican City — the Roman Curia — which act in the name and by authority of the Pope.

Incardination: The affiliation of a priest to his diocese. Every secular priest must belong to a certain diocese. Similarly, every priest of a religious community must belong to some jurisdiction of his community; this affiliation, however, is not called incardination.

Infallibility: (1) The inability of the Church to err in its teaching, in that she preserves and teaches the deposit of truth as revealed by Christ; (2) The inability of the Roman Pontiff to err when he teaches *ex cathedra* in matters of faith or morals, and indicates that the doctrine is to be believed by all the faithful; and (3) the inability of the college of bishops to err when speaking in union with the Pope in matters of faith and morals, agreeing that a doctrine must be held by the universal Church, and the doctrine is promulgated by the Pontiff.

Inquisition: A tribunal for dealing with heretics, authorized by Gregory IX in 1231 to search them out, hear and judge them, sentence them to various forms of punishment, and in some cases to hand them over to civil authorities for punishment. The Inquisition was a creature of its time when crimes against faith, which threatened the good of the Christian community, were regarded also as crimes against the state, and when heretical doctrines of such extremists as the Cathari and Albigensians threatened the very fabric of society. The institution, which was responsible for many excesses, was most active in the second half of the 13th century.

Instruction: A document containing doctrinal explanations, directive norms, rules, recommendations, admonitions, issued by the Pope, a department of the Roman Curia or other competent authority in the Church. To the extent that they so prescribe, instructions have the force of law.

Interdict: A censure imposed on persons for certain violations of church law. Interdicted persons may not take part in certain liturgical services, administer or receive certain sacraments.

Jurisdiction: Right, power, authority to rule. Jurisdiction in the Church is of divine institution; has pastoral service for its purpose; includes legislative, judicial, and executive authority; can be exercised only by persons with the power of orders. (1) Ordinary jurisdiction is attached to ecclesiastical offices by law; the officeholders, called Ordinaries, have authority over those who are subject to them. (2) Delegated jurisdiction is that which is granted to persons rather than attached to offices. Its extent depends on the terms of the delegation.

Keys, Power of the: Spiritual authority and jurisdiction in the Church, symbolized by the keys of the kingdom of heaven. Christ promised the keys to St. Peter, as head-to-be of the Church (Mt. 16:19), and commissioned him with full pastoral responsibility to feed his lambs and sheep (Jn. 21:15-17), The Pope, as the successor of St. Peter, has this power in a primary and supreme manner. The bishops of the Church also have the power, in union with and subordinate to the Pope. Priests share in it through holy orders and the delegation of authority. Examples of the application of the Power of the Keys are the exercise of teaching and pastoral authority by the Pope and bishops, the absolving of sins in the sacrament of penance, the granting of indulgences, the imposing of spiritual penalties on persons who commit certain serious sins.

Laicization: The process by which a man ordained to holy orders is relieved of the obligations of orders and the ministry and is returned to the status of a lay person.

Liberation Theology: Deals with the relevance of Christian faith and salvation — and, therefore, of the mission of the Church — to efforts for the promotion of human rights, social justice and human development. It originated in the religious, social, political and economic environment of Latin America, with its contemporary need for a theory and corresponding action by the Church, in the pattern of its overall mission, for human rights and integral personal and social development. Some versions of liberation theology are at variance with the body of church teaching because of their ideological concept of Christ as liberator, and also because they play down the primary spiritual nature and mission of the Church. Instructions from the Congregation for the

Doctrine of the Faith — "On Certain Aspects of the Theology of Liberation" (Sept. 3, 1984) and "On Christian Freedom and Liberation" (Apr. 5, 1986) — contain warnings against translating sociology into theology and advocating violence in social activism.

Magisterium: The Church's teaching authority, instituted by Christ and guided by the Holy Spirit, which seeks to safeguard and explain the truths of the faith. The Magisterium is exercised in two ways. The extraordinary Magisterium is exercised when the Pope and ecumenical councils infallibly define a truth of faith or morals that is necessary for one's salvation and that has been constantly taught and held by the Church. Ordinary Magisterium is exercised when the Church infallibly defines truths of the Faith as taught universally and without dissent; which must be taught or the Magisterium would be failing in its duty; is connected with a grave matter of faith or morals; and which is taught authoritatively. Not everything taught by the Magisterium is done so infallibly; however, the exercise of the Magisterium is faithful to Christ and what He taught.

Millennium: A thousand-year reign of Christ and the just upon earth before the end of the world. This belief of the Millenarians, Chiliasts, and some sects of modern times is based on an erroneous interpretation of Rv. 20.

Mission: (1) Strictly, it means being sent to perform a certain work, such as the mission of Christ to redeem mankind, the mission of the Apostles and the Church and its members to perpetuate the prophetic, priestly and royal mission of Christ. (2) A place where: the Gospel has not been proclaimed; the Church has not been firmly established; the Church, although established, is weak. (3) An ecclesiastical territory with the simplest kind of canonical organization, under the jurisdiction of the Congregation for the Evangelization of Peoples. (4) A church or chapel without a resident priest. (5) A special course of sermons and spiritual exercises conducted in parishes for the purpose of renewing and deepening the spiritual life of the faithful and for the conversion of lapsed Catholics.

Modernism: The "synthesis of all heresies," which appeared near the beginning of the 20th century. It undermines the objective validity of religious beliefs and practices which, it contends, are products of the subconscious developed by mankind under the stimulus of a religious sense. It holds that the existence of a personal God cannot be demonstrated, the Bible is not inspired, Christ is not divine, nor did he establish the Church or institute the sacraments. A special danger lies in modernism, which is still influential, because it uses Catholic terms with perverted meanings. St. Pius X condemned 65 propositions of modernism in 1907 in the decree *Lamentabili* and issued the encyclical *Pascendi* to explain and analyze its errors.

Monastery: The dwelling place, as well as the community thereof, of monks belonging to the Benedictine and Benedictine-related orders like the Cistercians and Carthusians; also, the Augustinians and Canons Regular. Distinctive of monasteries are: their separation from the world; the enclosure or cloister; the permanence or stability of attachment characteristic of their members; autonomous government in accordance with a monastic rule, like that of St. Benedict in the West or of St. Basil in the East; the special dedication of its members to the community celebration of the liturgy as well as to work that is suitable to the surrounding area and the needs of its people. Monastic superiors of men have such titles as abbot and prior; of women, abbess and prioress. In most essentials, an abbey is the same as a monastery.

Motu Proprio: A Latin phrase designating a document issued by a Pope on his own initiative. Documents of this kind often concern administrative matters.

Neo-Scholasticism: A movement begun in the late 19th century that had as its aim the restoration of Scholasticism for use in contemporary philosophy and theology. Great emphasis was placed upon the writings of such Scholastic masters as Peter Lombard, St. Albert the Great, St. Anselm, St. Bonaventure, Bl. John Duns Scotus, and especially St. Thomas Aquinas. The movement began at the Catholic University of Louvain, in Belgium, and then found its way into theological centers in Italy, France, and Germany. Particular attention was given to the philosophical and theological works of St. Thomas Aquinas, from which arose a particular school of neo-Thomism; the movement was strongly reinforced by Pope Leo XIII who issued the encyclical *Aeterni Patris* (1879) mandating that Scholasticism, in particular Thomism, be the foundation for all Catholic philosophy and theology taught in Catholic seminaries, universities, and colleges. Neo-Scholasticism was responsible for a true intellectual renaissance in 20th-century Catholic philosophy and theology. Among its foremost modern leaders were Jacques Maritain, Étienne Gilson, M. D. Chenu, Henri de Lubac, Yves Simon, and Paul Claudel.

Novemdiales: The nine days of official mourning that are held after the death of the Pope. They are to take place sequentially during the period between the death of the pontiff and the start of the conclave.

Ordination: The consecration of sacred ministers for divine worship and the service of people in things pertaining to God. The power of ordination comes from Christ and the Church, and must be conferred by a minister capable of communicating it.

Pallium: A band of white wool worn over the shoulders by all metropolitan archbishops and the Pope. The pallium is normally decorated with six black crosses and is made from the wool of two lambs blessed in the Church of St. Agnes in Rome. It is a symbol of union with the Holy See. Pope John Paul I was invested with the pallium at his installation in 1978, and John Paul II adopted the custom. Pope Benedict XVI was invested with a pallium adorned with five red crosses (symbolizing the wounds of Christ).

Papabile (also *Papabili*, pl.): An Italian word meaning essentially, "popeable." It is used to describe a Cardinal who is considered a strong possible candidate to become the next Pope.

Papal Election: The Pope is elected by the College of Cardinals during a secret conclave which begins no sooner than 15 days and no later than 20 days after the death of his predecessor. Cardinals under the age of 80, totaling no more than 120, are eligible to take part in the election by secret ballot. Election is by a two-thirds vote of participating Cardinals. New legislation regarding papal elections and church government during a vacancy of the Holy See was promulgated by Pope John Paul II on Feb. 23, 1996, in the apostolic constitution *Universi Dominici Gregis* ("Shepherd of the Lord's Whole Flock").

Patriarchs: (1) The leaders of the Israelite tribes and heads of prominent families who appear in Genesis from Adam to Joseph. Among the most significant patriarchs of the Old Testament are Abraham, Isaac, and Jacob; the patriarchal narratives in Genesis associated with them constitute the prologue to Israel's salvation history, and the period during which they lived is known as the Age of the Patriarchs. It is to be noted that the title of patriarch that was used for David (Acts 2:29) was simply one of honor. (2) The head of a branch of the Eastern Church, corresponding to a province of the one-time Roman Empire. There are five official traditional patriarchal sees: Rome, Constantinople, Alexandria, Antioch, and Jerusalem. Presently, the autocephalous churches of the Orthodox Church comprise several of these traditional patriarchates.

Pectoral Cross: A cross worn on a chain about the neck and over the breast by bishops and abbots as a mark of their office.

People of God: A name for the Church in the sense that it is comprised by a people with Christ as its head, the Holy Spirit as the condition of its unity, the law of love as its rule, and the kingdom of God as its destiny. Although it is a scriptural term, it was given new emphasis by the Second Vatican Council's Dogmatic Constitution on the Church (*Lumen Gentium*).

Pope: A title from the Italian word *papa* (from Greek *pappas*, father) used for the Bishop of Rome, the Vicar of Christ and successor of St. Peter, who exercises universal governance over the Church.

Relativism: Theory which holds that all truth, including religious truth, is relative, i.e., not absolute, certain or unchanging; a product of agnosticism, indifferentism, and an unwarranted extension of the notion of truth in positive science. Relativism is based on the tenet that certain knowledge of any and all truth is impossible. Therefore, no religion, philosophy or science can be said to possess the real truth; consequently, all religions, philosophies and sciences may be considered to have as much or as little of truth as any of the others.

Ring: In the Church a ring is worn as part of the insignia of bishops, abbots, et al.; by sisters to denote their consecration to God and the Church. The wedding ring symbolizes the love and union of husband and wife.

***Rogito*:** The official notarial act or document testifying to the burial of a Pope.

Scholasticism: The term usually applied to the Catholic theology and philosophy which developed in the Middle Ages.

Secularism: A school of thought, a spirit and manner of action which ignores and/or repudiates the validity or influence of supernatural religion with respect to individual and social life.

***Sede Vacante*:** The Latin term, meaning "vacant see," that is used for the papal interregnum. During the *sede vacante*, all formal official business in the governance of the Church ceases and resumes again only after the election of the new Pope. During the *sede vacante*, day-to-day administration of the Church is in the hands of the *Camerlengo* and the College of Cardinals.

Seminary: A house of study and formation for men, called seminarians, preparing for the priesthood. Traditional seminaries date from the Council of Trent in the middle of the 16th century; before that time, candidates for the priesthood were variously trained in monastic schools, universities under church auspices, and in less formal ways.

Suspension: A censure by which a cleric is forbidden to exercise some or all of his powers of orders and jurisdiction, or to accept the financial support of his benefices.

Synod, Diocesan: Meeting of representative persons of a diocese — priests, religious, lay persons — with the bishop, called by him for the purpose of considering and taking action on matters affecting the life and mission of the Church in the diocese. Persons taking part in a synod have consultative status; the bishop alone is the legislator, with power to authorize synodal decrees. According to canon law, every diocese should have a synod every 10 years.

Te Deum: The opening Latin words, *Thee, God*, of a hymn of praise and thanksgiving prescribed for use in the Office of Readings of the Liturgy of the Hours on many Sundays, solemnities, and feasts.

Theology: Knowledge of God and religion, deriving from and based on the data of divine revelation, organized and systematized according to some kind of scientific method. It involves systematic study and presentation of the truths of divine revelation in Sacred Scripture, tradition, and the teaching of the Church. Theology has been divided under various subject headings. Some of the major fields have been: dogmatic (systematic theology), moral, pastoral, historical, ascetical (the practice of virtue and means of attaining holiness and perfection), sacramental, and mystical (higher states of religious experience). Other subject headings include ecumenism (Christian unity, interfaith relations), ecclesiology (the nature and constitution of the Church), and Mariology (doctrine concerning the Blessed Virgin Mary), etc.

Thomism: The philosophy based on St. Thomas Aquinas (1224/5-1274), which is mandated to be the dominant philosophy used in Catholic educational institutions.

Titular Sees: Dioceses where the Church once flourished but which now exist only in name or title. Bishops without a territorial or residential diocese of their own — e.g., auxiliary bishops — are given titular sees. There are more than 2,000 titular sees; 16 of them are in the United States.

Universi Dominici Gregis: The 1996 Apostolic Constitution issued by Pope John Paul II to govern the rules and regulations for the next conclave. The constitution was followed in the conclave of 2005 and will remain in force until such time as it is superseded by another set of regulations, if a future pontiff chooses to issue one.

Urbi et Orbi: A Latin phrase meaning "To the City and to the World" that is a blessing given by the Holy Father. Normally, the first *Urbi et Orbi* delivered by a pontiff is immediately after his election by the College of Cardinals. This is a blessing accompanied by a short address to the crowds in St. Peter's Square and to the world; frequently, as with Pope John Paul II in 1978, it is delivered in as many languages as possible. The Pope also delivers an *Urbi et Orbi* each year at Christmas and at Easter.

Veni Creator Spiritus: A Latin phrase, meaning "Come, Creator Spirit" that is part of a hymn sung to the Holy Spirit. The hymn invokes the presence of the Holy Spirit and was perhaps first composed by Rabanus Maurus (776-856). The hymn is commonly sung as part of the Divine Office, papal elections, episcopal consecrations, ordinations, councils, synods, canonical elections, and confirmations.

Vocation: A call to a way of life. Generally, the term applies to the common call of all persons, from God, to holiness and salvation. Specifically, it refers to particular states of life, each called a vocation, in which response is made to this universal call: viz., marriage, the religious life and/or priesthood, the single state freely chosen or accepted for the accomplishment of God's will. The term also applies to the various occupations in which persons make a living. The Church supports the freedom of each individual to choose a particular vocation, and reserves the right to pass on the acceptability of candidates for the priesthood and religious life. Signs or indicators of particular vocations are many, including a person's talents and interests, circumstances and obligations, invitations of grace and willingness to respond thereto.

Vow: A promise made to God with sufficient knowledge and freedom, which has as its object a moral good that is possible and better than its voluntary omission. A person who professes a vow binds himself or herself by the virtue of religion to fulfill the promise. The best known examples of vows are those of poverty, chastity and obedience professed by religious. Public vows are made before a competent person, acting as an agent of the Church, who accepts the profession in the name of the Church, thereby giving public recognition to the person's dedication and consecration to God and divine worship. Vows of this kind are either solemn, rendering all contrary acts invalid as well as unlawful; or simple, rendering contrary acts unlawful. Solemn vows are for life; simple vows are for a definite period of time or for life. Vows professed without public recognition by the Church are called private vows. The Church, which has authority to accept and give public recognition to vows, also has authority to dispense persons from their obligations for serious reasons.

Zucchetto: A small skullcap worn by ecclesiastics, most notably prelates, and derived from the popular Italian vernacular term *zucca*, meaning a pumpkin, and used as slang for head. The Holy Father wears a white zucchetto made of watered silk; Cardinals use scarlet, and bishops use purple. Priests of the monsignorial rank may wear black with purple piping. All others may wear simple black.

Our Sunday Visitor ...
Your Source for Discovering the Riches of the Catholic Faith

Our Sunday Visitor has an extensive line of materials for young children, teens, and adults. Our books, Bibles, pamphlets, CD-ROMs, audios, and videos are available in bookstores worldwide.

To receive a FREE full-line catalog or for more information, call **Our Sunday Visitor** at **1-800-348-2440, ext. 3**. Or write **Our Sunday Visitor** / 200 Noll Plaza / Huntington, IN 46750.

Please send me ___ A catalog
Please send me materials on:
___ Apologetics and catechetics
___ Prayer books
___ The family
___ Reference works
___ Heritage and the saints
___ The parish

Name _____
Address _____ Apt._____
City _____ State _____ Zip_____
Telephone (   ) _____
                                                                        A53BBBBP

Please send a friend ___ A catalog
Please send a friend materials on:
___ Apologetics and catechetics
___ Prayer books
___ The family
___ Reference works
___ Heritage and the saints
___ The parish

Name _____
Address _____ Apt._____
City _____ State _____ Zip_____
Telephone (   ) _____
                                                                        A53BBBBP

OurSundayVisitor

200 Noll Plaza, Huntington, IN 46750
Toll free: **1-800-348-2440**
Website: www.osv.com